MW00526390

Pilgrim Journey

Pilgrim Journey

Instruction in
the Mystery of the Gospel

CURTIS W. FREEMAN

FORTRESS PRESS
MINNEAPOLIS

PILGRIM JOURNEY
Instruction in the Mystery of the Gospel

All Scripture quotations, unless otherwise indicated, are from New
Revised Standard Version Bible, copyright © 1989 National Council
of the Churches of Christ in the United States of America. Used by
permission. All rights reserved worldwide.
Scripture quotations marked (KJV) are from the King James Version,
public domain.
Scripture quotations marked (NKJV) are from the New King James
Version®. Copyright © 1982 by Thomas Nelson. Used by permission.
All rights reserved.

Library of Congress Control Number: 2023933164 (print)

Cover image: Illustrations to John Bunyan's "The Pilgrim's Progress."
William Blake, Christian Reading in His Book, Object 2 (Butlin
829.2), 17.2 x 12.6 cm

Cover design: Savanah N. Landerholm

Print ISBN: 978-1-5064-9490-6
eBook ISBN: 978-1-5064-9491-3

For

<small>THOSE WHO HAVE BEGUN THE</small>

<small>PILGRIM JOURNEY IN THE WATERS OF BAPTISM</small>

Think of us in this way: as servants of Christ and stewards of God's mysteries.

1 CORINTHIANS 4:1

Contents

Preface

IN AN ARTICLE PUBLISHED in the *Atlantic* in October 2021, journalist and former presidential speechwriter Peter Wehner wrestled with the question of why so much of American Christianity simply reflects the divisiveness of the wider culture. Churches have politicized the gospel, reinforced tribal identities, nurtured fears, and sacralized ugliness. In search of perspective, Wehner asked several prominent Christian leaders how this happened. James Ernest, vice president of William B. Eerdmans Publishing Company, offered a sobering assessment: "What we're seeing is massive discipleship failure caused by massive catechesis failure."[1] How could American Christians have failed so miserably to make disciples? If Ernest is correct, and I think he is, the heart of the problem is that churches have largely abandoned the historic practice of catechesis, of making Christians by personal instruction in the basic teaching of Christ. The results of this failure are catastrophic. The void left by the absence of basic Christian instruction has been filled by political, educational, and technological cultures.

Evangelical theologian J. I. Packer shares this assessment of the current crisis. He argues, "Where wise catechesis has flourished, the church has flourished. Where it has been neglected, the church has floundered."[2] The validation of this judgment seems self-evident. The church in America is floundering. Packer suggests two reasons for the loss of catechesis: the modern cultural rejection of authority and the resistance to authoritative instruction within Christian communities.[3] Yet there may be an even simpler reason for the loss of catechesis by Protestant congregations—Sunday school. As Christian education replaced Christian formation, developmental psychology superseded baptismal theology. The aim of Sunday school was not preparation for baptism and discipleship but rather the presentation of age-appropriate educational material, with the goal of gradual conversion to the faith. Among Evangelical Christians and other Free Church Protestants, this developmental model in the Sunday school hour was often followed by an evangelistic and revivalist theology in the worship service, where children were urged to make an immediate decision for Christ and come forward during the singing of an invitation hymn. The theological whiplash from this confused and conflicted process of gradual versus dramatic Christian formation was traumatic, but the upshot was that many Christians in America were simply inoculated with a weak strain of Christianity that rendered them immune to the real thing. The result left them unprotected from the virulent mutation that is now devouring American Christianity.

The good news is there is a growing movement seeking to retrieve the ancient ecumenical practice of Christian catechesis. The recovery of the catechetical tradition can be traced to the Second Vatican Council (1962–65), which called for the restoration of the catechumenate.[4] That call led to the production of the *Rite of Christian Initiation of Adults* (RCIA) for Catholic catechesis, which was formally approved for use in the United States in 1974.[5] Protestants began adapting the

RCIA and publishing their own catechetical materials. My book *Pilgrim Letters* was an effort in retrieving the practice of catechesis based on the six principles of the basic teaching of Christ described in Hebrews 6:1–2.[6] Along the way in the process of writing, I discovered the Institute for the Renewal of Christian Catechesis (IRCC), which maintains a website with excellent resources for catechesis across the Christian traditions.[7] I am grateful for the encouragement and collaboration of the IRCC and its director, Alex Fogleman, who invited me to join their team as a research fellow. I share the IRCC mission of recovering the ancient art of catechesis as a way of handing on the faith (1 Cor 11:2, 23). While instruction in the basic teaching of Christ may not be an immediate cure for the soul sickness of American Christianity, perhaps it may be more like a vaccination that inoculates those who desire to follow Christ and prevents them from contracting the spiritual disease that is endemic within the culture.

This book builds on the basic teaching of Christ and moves on to explore the mystery of the gospel. The theological and ecclesial outlook of *Pilgrim Journey,* like *Pilgrim Letters,* is evangelical and ecumenical, free church and catholic, ancient and future. There is, however, a difference. When I wrote *Pilgrim Letters,* I was able to draw on a long tradition of catechesis among Free Church Protestants with the aim of retrieving a lost practice. I am not aware of a similar tradition of mystagogy. Yet I hope this book will not only prove to be an exception but might also be a catalyst for more work about instruction in the mystery of the gospel.

Because Christianity has long enjoyed a dominant position in North America, the boundaries between church and culture have grown unclear and indistinct. It should not be surprising, then, that baptismal and post-baptismal catecheses were no longer seen as necessary for the mission of the church. For many, the presumption was that to be an American was to be a Christian or at least to live in a society that privileged and supported Christianity. This position of privilege meant that conversion did not require radical change. All that was necessary was a modest religious adjustment. The social situation in America has significantly shifted. One of the most glaring signs of Christian disestablishment is the rise of "the nones," people with no religious affiliation. In the 1970s, they were 5 percent of the US population, and now they are around 30 percent.[8] The decline of church membership, the loss of financial prosperity, and the lack of social influence have eroded the cultural establishment of Christianity and signal a future in which Christians must learn anew to practice the faith without privilege.

The bigger problem with the cultural accommodation of American Christianity is that it has lost a sense of the Christian life as a struggle, which was central to the catechetical practice of ancient Christianity. This struggle "begins with the humble fact that the church is not the world."[9] Becoming a Christian in the early church was not a simple matter. As one historian of early Christianity notes, "Conversion involved changes in belief, belonging, and behavior in the context of an experience with God."[10] In this book, I contend that we can best think about the future of the faith after we have gone back and examined the models of ancient Christianity.[11] It is a fool's gambit to think it is possible to leapfrog from the New Testament to now. We must look to patterns and practices among generations of earlier Christians in order to find models that we can recover and adapt for our current context.[12]

Unlike God, "with whom there is no variation or shadow due to change" (James 1:17), the wider social setting in which Christians live is mutable and unstable. In the apostolic age, Christians did not expect or receive support from the wider social culture. The front door of the church opened to the frontier of mission. In the fourth century, a new church-world arrangement began to emerge. This new arrangement was the Christendom paradigm. Christianity went from being a distinct community in a hostile environment to becoming an institution privileged and supported by the empire and its Christian rulers. As a result, the mission of the church became a kind of foreign policy of the state. The Christendom arrangement of church and world continued in various iterations through the centuries. We are living today in the midst of an emerging reality that looks more similar to the days of early Christianity than the longtime establishment of Christendom.[13]

Some Christians will respond to the changing times by putting their energy and effort in service of political processes and market forces. Others will return to the more secluded spaces of their own fellowship and refrain from encountering the wider church and culture. It is not clear that either of these alternatives can sustain a faithful or effective mission for the church. The way pursued in this book commends moving into the future by recovering ancient practices that form Christians who are prepared to engage the surrounding culture through the power of witness.[14] To do so, we must learn to "make Christians" who understand what it means to be part of an apostolic and apocalyptic community at the same time.[15] Such formation requires a bifocal vision, which sees that this is that and then is now:

> *This is that*: We are the apostolic community, and the
>   commands of Jesus are addressed to us.
> *Then is now*: We are the end-time people, a new
>   humanity anticipating the consummation of the
>   blessed hope.[16]

The conviction that "the church is not the world" is not a sectarian or restoration stance committed to the recovery of some version of naive primitivism. It is instead a commitment to making disciples by retrieving the ancient Christian practice of catechesis.

Catechesis is not about reaching a full understanding of the faith once delivered to the saints. Nor is it about encouraging Christians to think for themselves. It is about acquiring a basic elementary language. It is teaching Christians to speak Christian. As my colleague Stanley Hauerwas puts it, "You can only act in the world you can see, and you can only come to see what you can say."[17] Catechesis is the church giving us words to speak the convictions of our faith, and by helping baptismal candidates learn that speech, we provide them with a language to see what we say. Learning the grammar of the Christian faith is essential to seeing what we say. Catechetical instruction is evangelical and ecumenical, formational and educational, confessional and convictional. Catechesis is about making Christians by helping them learn to speak as Christians so that they might live as Christians.

Although Christian churches observed it differently over the first millennium, there were four recognizable stages of Christian initiation: (1) *separation*: entrance into the catechumenate; (2) *transition and preparation*: period of initiation and instruction; (3) *incorporation*: observance of baptism, confirmation, and first communion; and (4) *mystagogy*: instruction in the mysteries.[18] These four stages of Christian initiation marked four distinct phases of conversion, in which converts were regarded first as *seekers*, then as *hearers*, next as *kneelers*, and finally as *faithful*.[19] This ancient process provides a model for missional churches today to evangelize the unchurched, disciple new believers, equip maturing believers, and incorporate new members.[20]

When Saint Egeria traveled from her home in Spain to the Holy Land in the fourth century, she noted that catechumens received daily instruction during Lent followed by a week of instruction in the mysteries.[21] The focus of baptismal catechesis for Cyril the bishop of Jerusalem was biblical and doctrinal instruction, while the purpose of mystagogical instruction was to expound for newly baptized Christians the spiritual significance of baptism, anointing, Eucharist, and liturgy.[22] Recovering this ancient practice of instruction in the mysteries offers an opportunity to renew the life and mission of the church today. God has entrusted the church with the gift of holy mysteries to strengthen us in our earthly pilgrimage. These mysteries are sacred signs that proclaim the gospel of Jesus Christ. They are gifts that belong to all God's people, and by receiving instruction in the mysteries, we become stewards (1 Cor 4:1). To put it differently, faithful Christian discipleship entails the responsibility to make the mystery of the gospel central to the worship, work, and witness of the church.[23]

The purpose of mystagogical catechesis is to stimulate, strengthen, and sustain the understanding of the mystery of the gospel so that it leads to a more committed and mature practice of the Christian life. Because instruction in the mysteries is not only a matter of Christian education but also of spiritual formation, it is important that participants actively seek the available means of grace through prayer, worship, scripture, study, devotion, ministry, and service. The church is a pilgrim community that lives as exiles in the present age but journeys by faith to our true home.[24] Like Abraham, we are pilgrims on earth looking "forward to the city that has foundations, whose architect and builder is God" (Heb 11:10). This journey, however, is different from others. It lasts our entire lifetime and requires what Eugene Peterson described as "a long obedience in the same direction."[25] We remember that as Israel "had the manna to nourish them in the wilderness to Canaan; so have we the sacraments, to nourish us in the church, and in our wilderness-condition."[26]

At some point, readers may note that this instruction in the mysteries looks and sounds like basic Christian theology. They would be correct, for as historian Thomas M. Finn observed, "The theology of early Christians was the result of symbols deeply lived."[27] My hope in returning to the ancient practice of instruction in the mystery of the gospel is that it might foster greater reflection on these deeply lived symbols of the faith that unite us with Jesus Christ, the life of the world (John 1:4).

Finally, I wish to express my thanks to friends who have encouraged and sustained me in the process of writing: Paul Fiddes, Janet Soskice, David Lyle Jeffrey, Stephen Chapman, Stanley Hauerwas, Lauren Winner, Fred P. Edie, George Mason, Ellen Davis, Lester Ruth, Darryl Powell, and Debra Freeman, and to Caroline Hiler for preparing the indices. I also want to offer a special word of thanks to Carey Newman at Fortress Press, who welcomed and supported this project to publication. Their friendship models the discernment of the mystery that is the concern of this book. As theologian David Burrell reminds us, if there is truth to be had, it will be found through ongoing conversations "in a tradition, within a community, in the company of friends."[28]

CURTIS W. FREEMAN
ON THE FEAST OF JOHN BUNYAN
AUGUST 29, 2022

Figure 1

My name is Secret, I dwell with those that are high. . . . The merciful one has sent me to tell thee that he is a God ready to forgive, and that he taketh delight to multiply pardon to offences. He also would have thee know that he inviteth thee to come into his presence, to his Table and that he will feed thee with the Fat of his House, and with the Heritage of Jacob thy Father.[1]

Introduction

The Mystery Hidden through the Ages

DEAR PILGRIM:

When I wrote to you before, you were preparing for baptism. In those letters, I shared with you the basic teaching of Christ from the book of Hebrews about repentance, faith, baptism, the laying on of hands, resurrection, and eternal judgment (Heb 6:2). Those six principles lay an excellent foundation upon which to build as you continue to grow and mature as a follower of Christ. They are basic teachings, but there is much more to learn as you continue your journey. Now you are ready to "go on to perfection" (Heb 6:1) as you receive instruction in the mystery of the gospel.

I am sure you recognize the term *mystery* as a popular type of fictional literature. The mystery plot explores an event, typically a crime, that remains unexplained until the end of the story. The characters include a range of suspects with motive and opportunity and a protagonist who solves the mystery. The archetypal figure of the mystery novel is surely Sherlock Holmes, the fictional London detective in the stories of Sir Arthur Conan Doyle, who sorts out and solves seemingly insoluble problems with an ingenious combination of science, logic, and deduction. His investigation always follows the simple precept that "when you have eliminated the impossible, whatever remains, *however improbable*, must be the truth."[2]

Stories with a complicated plot and colorful characters compel our attention and provoke our curiosity, especially when they conclude with a dramatic ending where the problem is resolved with an improbable turn and an unexpected outcome. Yet Holmes signals that what we typically think of as a mystery is really a problem in disguise. As the Christian philosopher Gabriel Marcel famously noted, there is a fundamental difference between a problem and a mystery.[3] A problem presents itself complete before us, challenging our intellect to comprehend it, but a mystery is an unfolding reality that calls for our personal involvement to be grasped by it. A problem can be explained, but a mystery surpasses explanation. A mystery essentially invites the engagement of our whole being and evokes a sense of wonder in the search for truth. We never fully and completely understand a mystery. We only discern it in a partial and incomplete sense. Calling a problem a "mystery" does not make it so. Some problems, like global climate change, national healthcare, or pandemic diseases, are "wicked problems" because they are seemingly irresolvable. However, they are not mysteries because we approach them with the understanding that there is a solution.[4]

My basic aim in these letters is to help you gain a sense of what it means to believe that a mystery, not a problem, lies at the heart of the Christian faith. I have to confess that I did not always put the matter in quite this way. There was a time when I perceived God as a "problem" to sort out. I wondered whether it was possible, or even desirable, to believe in God.[5] I was not alone. Somewhat later, I came to read the letters of Simone Weil in which she described how as a young person she gave up on "the problem of God" as something that could not be solved. Nevertheless, she found herself compelled to embrace the mystery of God's reality, not because she was rationally convinced of God's existence but rather because while suffering from migraine headaches during Holy Week services, "the thought of the passion of Christ entered into [her] being once and for all."[6] She did not mean to diminish the importance of always being ready to make a defense to anyone who demands from us an accounting for the hope we have in Christ (1 Pet 3:15).

The search for a reasonable faith has a long and valued history among Christian theologians and philosophers, who often begin their treatises by reflecting on the arguments for the existence of God. Yet it is worth noting that the very notion of existence is itself problematic. God is not simply one being among others. God is the reality that makes possible the existence of everything that is. Rather than constructing arguments to prove that God *exists,* it seems better to say that God *is.* God spoke to Moses, saying, "I am who I am" (Exod 3:14). This statement suggests that what it is to be God is simply to be. There is no way to separate God's essence (who God is) from God's existence (the reality of God's being).[7] These reasoned accounts, however, seem to have lost their way over time as the defenders of theism increasingly ended up justifying the case for a Christian god without Christ.[8] Rather than showing that the Christian faith is reasonable, they left little room for faith beyond reason. One philosopher put the matter bluntly, describing "a theological paradox" as "what a contradiction becomes when it is about God rather than something else."[9]

The presumption that God is a problem to be solved rather than a mystery to be discerned rests on a misconception that God must conform to human ways of thinking. That simply does not fit the living God of Israel and Jesus Christ whom we meet in the Bible. As the prophet Isaiah declared:

> For my thoughts are not your thoughts,
>   nor are your ways my ways, says the Lord.
> For as the heavens are higher than the earth,
>   so are my ways higher than your ways
>   and my thoughts than your thoughts. (Isa 55:8–9)

Anselm, an eleventh-century theologian and archbishop of Canterbury, suggested that God by definition is "that thing than which nothing greater can be thought."[10] You might ask how we could even begin to describe a being whose thoughts and ways are greater than anything we can conceive. Theophilus, the second-century patriarch of Antioch, Syria, compared the limits of human understanding to the seeds of a pomegranate that cannot perceive anything beyond the rind. In the same way, he said, "Human beings who are enclosed with all creation in the hands of God cannot see God."[11]

We cannot know God the way we know other things. God remains hidden from the eyes of our mind and surpasses our thinking and understanding. The limits of our knowledge require that we approach the matter of knowing God differently. When we use the word "G-o-d," we are not naming a something in our immediate experience to which we can point. God is not a warm feeling in our heart or a still small voice speaking in our conscience. God is the ultimate source in which "we live and move and have our being" (Acts 17:28). The word "G-o-d" stands for the mystery of the world that surpasses our thinking and speaking.[12] To say that God is the mystery of the world is not a way of saying that God is simply the summation of all we know plus all we do not know. It is a shorthand for the conviction that God's thoughts and ways are not our thoughts and ways. God transcends us, not just in quantity but in quality. Yet to say that this mystery

we call God is inexpressible does not mean we can say nothing about God. Indeed, when we say that God is a mystery,
we are saying something. The Psalmist exclaims that God's
"knowledge is too wonderful for me; it is so high that I cannot
attain it" (Ps 139:6). This statement is not a concession that
human language about God is so inadequate we must remain
utterly silent before God. Rather, the recognition of God as
mystery moves us to praise God, although even our highest
praise cannot express the fullness of the glory God deserves.
Mystery, then, is both an expression in language about the
unlimited reality of God and a statement about the limits of
human language.[13]

Christian theologians have long maintained that even
though it is impossible to describe the hidden nature of God's
being, it is possible and permissible to speak of God by naming what God is not.[14] Return for a moment to God's self-
declaration that God's thoughts and ways are not our ways
and thoughts. Our thoughts are limited or finite, but God's
thoughts are not. That is what it means to say God is omni-
scient. It is not an equation of God's knowledge to all the data
on the Internet and in the libraries of the world. It is a way of
talking about God as one "unto whom all hearts are open, all
desires known, and from whom no secrets are hid."[15] Similarly,
our power is limited or finite, but God's power is not. That is
what it means to say God is omnipotent. It is not a foolish
claim that speculates about whether God can create a stone
so heavy that even God cannot lift it.[16] It simply affirms the
conviction that "for God all things are possible" (Mark 10:27;
Matt 19:26). Likewise, our ability to be present is limited and
finite in space and time, but God is not. It is important to
remember that as Christians, we cannot utter the word "God"
apart from the word "Jesus." The God who meets us in Christ
is not all-powerful in the sense of the unlimited capacity to
unleash strength and sovereignty. Rather, in Christ, we see

that God's "power is made perfect in weakness" (2 Cor 12:9). That is what it means to say God is omnipresent. It is not an absurd assertion that proposes God occupies all the physical space in the universe at once. It is a modest way of trying to confirm what it means to confess with the Psalmist:

> Where can I go from your spirit?
>   Or where can I flee from your presence?
> If I ascend to heaven, you are there;
>   if I make my bed in Sheol, you are there.
> If I take the wings of the morning
>   and settle at the farthest limits of the sea,
> even there your hand shall lead me,
>   and your right hand shall hold me fast.
> If I say, "Surely the darkness shall cover me,
>   and the light around me become night,"
> even the darkness is not dark to you;
>   the night is as bright as the day,
>   for darkness is as light to you. (Ps 139:7–12)

God is an all-knowing, all-powerful, and ever-present being. However, when we speak of God's omniscience, omnipotence, and omnipresence, we are not speculating about how much knowledge, power, or presence God really has. Knowledge of God's nature is simply not within our capacity to know. Speaking about God by saying what God is not is helpful because it restrains the human tendency to make God in our own image and reminds us that God is God, and we are not.[17] It serves to reinforce what the Psalmist says with simplicity and clarity: "Know that the Lord is God. It is [the Lord] that made us, and not we ourselves" (Ps 100:3).[18]

When I first began to think more deeply about the faith, I read a wonderful book called *Knowing God*. The author explained that the Christian calling is to know God, not just to know about God.[19] Yet God is a mystery that is beyond our capacity to know. All the images we use to imagine God, all the thoughts we have to conceive of God, all the words we utter to speak of God are inadequate and inappropriate to express the knowledge of God. As one theologian observed, God is "the Unknown by our knowing, the Unconceived by our concepts, the Measureless for our measures, the Inexperienceable for our experience."[20] We cannot know God on our own. As Karl Barth reminded us, "God is known by God and by God alone."[21] The good news is that the unknowable God chose to be known in Jesus Christ, the living Word of God, who speaks to us through the Bible, the written Word of God. The biblical story tells about "the mystery that has been hidden throughout the ages," which in Christ has been revealed to the people of God (Col 1:26–27). We can know God because God made Godself known in the life, death, and resurrection of Jesus. In him "are hidden all the treasures of wisdom and knowledge" (Col 2:3). In God's revelation in Christ, the incomprehensible God becomes apprehensible, not by sight but by faith (2 Cor 5:7). Jesus makes it possible to know God, which is not just a matter of the head. As one Christian philosopher put it, human beings are not just brains on a stick. We are creatures defined by what we desire.[22] To know God is to love God with all our heart, soul, strength, and mind (Luke 10:27). This holistic and integral way of knowing is surely what the apostle Paul was getting at when he said, "I regard everything as loss because of the surpassing value of knowing Christ Jesus my Lord" (Phil 3:8).

My earlier book of letters to you concluded with a reflection on the admonition to "go on to perfection" (Heb 6:1). You will remember I said that the purpose of the Christian life is to continue growing spiritually into wholeness and maturity. Receiving instruction in the basic teaching of Christ is only the beginning. Continuing the pilgrim journey requires instruction in the mystery of the gospel. In the language of the early church, *mystagogy* must follow *catechesis*. Gregory of Nyssa, the fourth-century bishop of Cappadocia, shows how the life of Moses exemplifies what going on to perfection looks like. One day while Moses was tending the flock of his father-in-law, he encountered a great mystery. God spoke from a burning bush. Moses listened and obeyed the word of God, trusted in the power of God over Pharaoh's army, led the people of Israel out of Egypt, and crossed through the waters of the Red Sea and into the wilderness, where God sustained them with food and drink. Gregory suggests that the life of Moses serves as a spiritual model of how catechetical instruction leads from faith to baptism followed by spiritual nourishment through word, sacrament, and prayer (1 Cor 10:1–4). His mystagogic instruction, however, did not occur until Moses ascended Mount Sinai, where he "entered the darkness and then saw God in it" (Ex 20:21).[23] There in the cloud that hid God on the mountain, Moses saw God, not with his physical eyes but with the spiritual eyes of his soul. In the darkness, he could not comprehend with his rational sense the unknowable mystery, but he did apprehend with a spiritual sense the splendor of God's dwelling place in all its glory.[24]

The purpose of this instruction is not so you will understand the mystery but rather that you might learn to discern it.[25] Even when you find it difficult, you must learn to "hold fast to the mystery of the faith with a clear conscience" (1 Tim 3:9). It is a wonderful treasure that sustains and supports "the household of God, which is the church of the living God, the pillar and bulwark of the truth" (1 Tim 3:15). As you continue your journey, never forget that at the center of our life together is the great mystery of God in Christ:

> He was revealed in flesh,
>   vindicated in spirit,
>   seen by angels,

proclaimed among Gentiles,
  believed in throughout the world,
    taken up in glory. (1 Tim 3:16)

The unseeable, unknowable, unspeakable mystery hidden through the ages became seen, known, and heard in the life, death, and resurrection of Jesus of Nazareth. The apostle John testifies,

> We declare to you what was from the beginning, what we have heard, what we have seen with our eyes, what we have looked at and touched with our hands, concerning the word of life—this life was revealed, and we have seen it and testify to it, and declare to you the eternal life that was with the Father and was revealed to us—we declare to you what we have seen and heard so that you also may have fellowship with us; and truly our fellowship is with the Father and with his Son Jesus Christ. (1 John 1:1–3)

Yet even in this revelation, God and God's ways remain a deep mystery. As the poet William Cowper wrote in the hymn,

> God moves in a mysterious way,
> His wonders to perform.
> He plants his footsteps in the sea,
> And rides upon the storm.[26]

The letters that follow explore seven mysteries of the faith: the one Word of God, the two testaments of Christian Scripture, the three persons of the Holy Trinity, the four senses of biblical reasoning, the five acts of God's story, the six seasons of the Christian year, and the seven sacramental signs of God's presence. Your reception of these mysteries may not lead you to a heightened mystic communion like Gregory of Nyssa described. Nevertheless, with this instruction, you will become a steward of the mysteries (1 Cor 4:1). These mysteries are not problems or puzzles to pry into. Cyril of Jerusalem cautioned that if anyone who has not received the basic instruction of Christ asks about the teaching, the steward is to say nothing. For the mysteries of the faith are for those who believe and have been enlightened through teaching of the gospel.[27] You will be entrusted with special responsibility for the mysteries. They belong to the whole church, but you will become a steward of them. Guard them prayerfully and teach them faithfully so the church may be blessed, "for all things are yours, . . . and you are Christ's, and Christ is God's" (1 Cor 3:21, 23, NKJV).

At the beginning of each letter, there is an image from the poet and artist William Blake and an epigraph from *The Pilgrim's Progress* by preacher and author John Bunyan. You will remember that the images and story of Blake and Bunyan provided a visual and narrative shape for our previous correspondence. I continue that pattern in these letters. I have made some slight adjustments. These inscriptions are drawn from the second part of *The Pilgrim's Progress* that tells of the journey of Christian's wife, Christiana, and their four sons from the City of Destruction to the Celestial City. Although Blake provided illustrations from scenes in part one of *The Pilgrim's Progress*, he made none for part two. I have selected images from the substantial archive of illustrations Blake made for other works that fit the theme of each letter. The picture above (figure 1) shows Los, who personifies the faculty of imaginative creativity, passing through the gothic archway of a church, suggesting the beginning of his journey in search of true faith.[28] His sandaled feet mark him as a prophet, and the lantern in his right hand shines like a miniature sun to guide him through the darkness. As Blake tells us, "Los took his globe of fire to search the interior of Albion's bosom."[29] In the selected quote from *The Pilgrim's Progress*, Secret, representing God's intimate knowledge of and concern for a personal experience of grace, announces that the mysterious and merciful One stands ready to forgive and to welcome her into the divine presence. God promises to sustain her with spiritual food for the journey. It is assurance to us as well as we continue on our pilgrim journey.

Yours in discerning the mystery,

Interpreter

Figure 2

Now the Glass was one of a thousand. It would present a man, one way, with his own Feature exactly, and turn it but another way, and it would shew one the very Face and Similitude of the Prince of Pilgrims himself. Yea I have talked with them that can tell, and they have said, that they have seen the very Crown of Thorns upon his Head, by looking in that Glass, they have therein also seen the holes in his Hands, in his Feet, and his Side.[1]

Mystery 1

One Word: Jesus Christ

Dear Pilgrim:

The first great mystery of the Christian faith holds that "God was in Christ, reconciling the world unto himself" (2 Cor 5:19, KJV). This mystery is impossible for us *to figure out*, but by speaking to us, God has made it possible for us *to find out*. The opening scene of the Bible describes the creation of heaven and earth. "The earth," we are told, "was a formless void and darkness covered the face of the deep" (Gen 1:2). Then God's Spirit began moving over the water, and God spoke into the silent darkness: "Let there be light" (Gen 1:3). Who God is and what God was doing before God spoke the universe into existence is hidden from us. Only God knows. Yet the invisible and unknowable God chose to become visible and known through speech. God's Word has always been with God. It is the personal expression of God's own being (John 1:1–2). God's Word is the life and light of all things (John 1:3–5). The Word that was with God from before time entered the world through a human life—Jesus, the "one and the same Son" who is the eternal Word of God (John 1:14).[2]

The great twentieth-century theologian Karl Barth explained that we encounter God's Word in a threefold form: spoken, written, and living.[3] When *the spoken Word* proclaims Christ, God speaks. Preaching that bears faithful witness to the revelation of God in Christ is not just a matter of talking about God. In it, God talks to us. God has chosen to use preaching as a means to communicate the good news (1 Cor 1:21; Rom 10:14, 17). In this sense, Christian proclamation is the Word of God that makes known the mystery revealed in Christ (Col 1:25–28; 2:2; 4:3). We also confront God's Word in the Bible. *The written Word* is inspired by God (2 Tim 3:16), and its human authors were moved by the Spirit to speak from God (2 Pet 1:20–21). Scripture is the Word of God because it speaks to us and is heard by us as God's Word but most importantly because it bears witness to God's self-disclosure in *the living Word*, Jesus Christ, the Word made flesh (John 1:14). Yet these three forms of God's Word are not three different Words. For there is only one Word of God, Jesus Christ, to whom Christian proclamation witnesses and Christian Scripture attests. Belief in the incarnation of the Word rests on the conviction that God came and comes in the person of Jesus Christ. As Ignatius of Antioch testified, "God is one, and he has revealed himself in his Son Jesus Christ, who is his Word issuing from the silence."[4]

Yet even in the revelation of God's Word in Jesus, the mystery remains. Although God is revealed in Christ, God is also hidden in Christ. The mystery is both disclosed and veiled. Maximus the Confessor, the seventh-century Christian theologian, observed:

> The incarnation is a mystery even more inconceivable than any other. By taking flesh God makes himself understood only by appearing still more incomprehensible. He remains hidden . . . even in this disclosure. Even when manifest he is always the stranger.[5]

The hiddenness of God is not simply a consequence of the limits of human knowledge. God is hidden because God chooses to hide. As the prophet Isaiah observed, "Truly, you are a God who hides himself, O God of Israel, the Savior" (Isa 45:15). Martin Luther suggested that if God intentionally withholds aspects of the divine will and ways from us, we ought to focus our attention on what God has revealed rather than speculating about the inscrutable hiddenness of God that God has not revealed.[6] Yet as Luther also cautiously noted, when we focus our attention on God's revelation in Christ, we confront a hidden presence. God hides in plain sight. That the God who speaks in Christ remains unknown to so many is not because they cannot understand God's Word but instead because they refuse to believe the scandalous news of a God who suffers and dies on a cross, who says, "My power is made perfect in weakness" (2 Cor 2:9). As a result, they worship an idol of their own making rather than the One who is the Maker of heaven and earth. When we contemplate the revelation of God in Christ, we behold the majesty and glory of God manifested, not in dominion and dominance but in vulnerability and weakness.[7]

The Fourth Ecumenical Council of 451 CE offered the classic doctrinal formulation of the mystery of the incarnation. The Creed of Chalcedon affirms the deity and humanity of Christ as two natures existing in one person. It describes the two natures as separate and distinct yet united so that they are unconfused, unchangeable, indivisible, and inseparable as "one and the same Son, the only-begotten, God the Word, the Lord Jesus Christ."[8] The Chalcedonian formula conveyed the basic conviction that all humanity shared with Jesus the same human nature and thus participated in the benefits of the incarnation, while it also maintained that the human nature of Jesus is the personhood of the Son of God, and thus the two natures exist together.[9] The Chalcedonian doctrine does not explain the mystery of the incarnation. Instead, it offers careful language that has enabled Christians to declare the faith proclaimed since the days of the apostles, that in Jesus Christ "all the fullness of God was pleased to dwell" (Col 1:19). This conviction is central to the language of the Chalcedonian formula.

The confessional statements of many Protestant Christians have tended to echo the language of Chalcedon, although it is not always clear how these doctrinal declarations relate to the practical expressions of the faith. For example, the confession accepted by the New Connection Baptists in 1770 alluded to the Chalcedonian formulation, not because it seemed essential to their faith but because they believed it to be the plain teaching of Scripture:

> We believe, that our Lord Jesus Christ is God and man, united in one person: or possessed of divine perfection united to human nature, in a way which we pretend not to explain, but think ourselves bound by the word of God firmly to believe.[10]

Evangelical Protestants have tended to stress the priority of a personal confession of faith more than corporate confession of faith, though recognizing that both are necessary. They see the apostolic pattern in the confession of the apostle Peter, "You are the Messiah, the Son of the living God" (Matt 16:16); and the apostle John, "My Lord and my God!" (John 20:28); and the apostle Paul, "If you confess with your lips that Jesus is Lord and believe in your heart that God raised him from the dead, you will be saved" (Rom 10:9).

The key point to remember is that the incarnation is not a problem to explain or a riddle to solve. It is a mystery to receive and to discern. The theological grammar of the creeds provides careful language for talking about the incarnation. It offers us a way of speaking about the Word, who "for us humans and for our salvation came down from the heavens and became incarnate from the Holy Spirit and the Virgin Mary."[11] The underlying conviction of the formula that *God was in Christ reconciling the world* has endured, even though the theological formulation of *two natures existing in one person* has often proved challenging to adapt in different contexts and to new ways of thinking.

Early in my theological explorations, I read the book *God Was in Christ* by the Scottish theologian D. M. Baillie. He suggested that the way to make sense of the affirmation of Jesus as both divine and human is to recognize the incarnation as a *paradox*, which he explained requires affirming "two contradictory, logically incompatible, but ontologically necessary assertions."[12] He compared the language of the two-natures doctrine to a world map that stretches and distorts the round shape of the globe to flatten it onto the page so that the size and shape of Greenland at the top of the map is exaggerated. This way of describing the incarnation maintains the conviction that Jesus was both human and divine, but it does not offer much help in accounting for the union of the two natures in Christ. My colleague Jeremy Bebgie, a theologian and pianist, often asks students to consider the seemingly impossible notion of two natures in one person by sounding middle C on a piano and then depressing without sounding the C one octave higher. Though only the first key is sounded, the second may be heard through the sympathetic resonance of the strings. He then asks how this musical phenomenon might help us to think about the mystery of the incarnation.

My theological mentor, Jim McClendon, proposed a two-narratives model as an alternative way of expressing the historic affirmation of Chalcedon: one story of God's self-giving and another story of divine fulfillment in human up-reaching. Jesus, McClendon declared, embodies both stories, and the gospel witness, he continued, attests to the conviction that these two are indivisibly one in Jesus—the "one and the same Son" who is the eternal word of God.[13] The affirmation that the human and divine stories are one in Jesus, however, does not mean he was simply the "lucky winner" adopted by God. As McClendon states, "There was never a time when God did not intend to raise Jesus from the dead, never a time when the whole story pointed to anything less than the ultimate exaltation of this One."[14] And though there are two stories, human and divine, "there is one storyteller, God, who acknowledges both stories as his own, who tells himself in both." Thus, the human story of Jesus is "grounded in the intentionality of the divine storyteller."[15]

Maps, music, and stories may be helpful analogies to better discern the mystery, but they underscore the challenges of believing what may seem unbelievable. It would be a mistake, however, to think of the incarnation as a doctrine that simply must be believed even if it cannot be understood. Discerning the mystery of God in Christ is essential because it provides insight into our salvation. Consider the prayer of Jesus in the garden of Gethsemane. Jesus asked the Father three times that the cup of suffering and death might pass from him, nevertheless deferring "not what I want but what you want" (Matt 26:39). Here the human will of Jesus appears to be in tension if not outright conflict with the divine will of the Father. We might wonder whether Jesus could have chosen to disobey. Later reformulations of the Chalcedonian formula, like that of Maximus the Confessor, have placed the christological question within a trinitarian framework, helping us to understand why Jesus could not choose or act contrary to the divine will. For in him God accomplished what the sons and daughters of earth, weakened by sinful flesh, could not do. God sent the eternal Son to share the same sinful human flesh as all those who dwell east of Eden, yet his will was not determined by bondage to the flesh but rather by his union with the eternal Son of God (Rom 8:3). It was not that Jesus as a human being was *not able to sin* but rather that by his union with the eternal Word, he was *able not to sin*.[16] As the book of Hebrews says, "Although he was a Son, he learned obedience through what he suffered; and having been made perfect, he became the source of eternal salvation for all who obey him" (Heb 5:8–9). The one who prayed in the Garden was not just the man Jesus of Nazareth but "one and the same Son, the only-begotten, God the Word, the Lord Jesus Christ." In praying "as You will," Jesus acted in willing just as all other humans act in willing. Yet his willing was not just *with* the Son but *as* the Son in union with the Father and the Spirit.[17]

Another way of discerning the mystery is through the threefold office of Christ. God's covenant with Israel was mediated through three types of leaders: prophet, priest, and king. Those who exercised their gifts in these roles served as ministers of the covenant, and each was anointed as a sign of consecration to their respective ministries. No one fulfilled all three offices, though some exercised more than one. Melchizedek was a king and a priest (Gen 14:18) but not a prophet. David was a prophet (2 Sam 23:2) and a king (2 Sam 7:12–16) but not a priest. Jeremiah was a priest and a prophet (Jer 1:1–2) but not a king. Yet all three were realized in one life: God's anointed, Jesus Christ. The Lord raised Jesus up as a prophet from among his own people and put words in his mouth (Deut 18:18). The Lord swore to him, saying, "You are a priest forever according to the order of Melchizedek" (Ps 110:4). The Lord designated him to rule as king and Son (Ps 2:6–7). Throughout history, the church has spoken of the threefold office of

Jesus Christ because he fulfilled all three offices as prophet, priest, and king. In him, these offices were transformed. He was a prophet who spoke the Word of the Lord, but different from any other, he was the incarnation of the Word that the prophet spoke (John 1:1–18). As the Great High Priest, he offered up the atoning sacrifice on behalf of all humanity. Yet he was not only the priest who offered the sacrifice; his own body was the sacrifice offered as atonement for sin (Heb 4:14). And he governs as King of kings and Lord of lords (Rev 19:16), yet he reigns not by the sword but through the cross, and as the humble and suffering servant, he has been given the name Lord and exalted to the right hand of the Father (Phil 2:5–11). By fulfilling all three offices in his life and ministry, Jesus Christ is the mediator of a new covenant. The fellowship between God and humanity that existed in creation and was disrupted by sin has been restored through Jesus Christ. The covenant that was established by God's promise and broken by the unfaithfulness of God's people has been renewed because "in Christ God was reconciling the world to himself" (2 Cor 5:19). In him, God has spoken the one word upon which the salvation of the world depends.[18]

The epigraph for this chapter comes from a scene in *The Pilgrim's Progress*, when Christiana and her fellow pilgrims are approaching the Delectable Mountains, from which travelers can see the Celestial City. The company arrives at the tents of the shepherds, who welcome them into their great house, where they share a meal together. The next morning, Mercy sees a looking glass in the dining room. She expresses a great desire to have it and wonders if the shepherds might be willing to give (or sell) it to her. Bunyan explains that anyone who looks into the great glass sees a perfect reflection of their own features but on changing the angle of gaze beholds the image of Jesus Christ, the Prince of Pilgrims. In the glass, Bunyan says, some can see the very crown of thorns on his head and the wounds in his hands, feet, and side. Those who fix their vision on the glass, which is the written Word, see him who is the living Word. Adding a marginal biblical reference, Bunyan indicates that there they see the glory of God "as though reflected in a mirror," and in seeing, they "are being transformed into the same image" (2 Cor 3:18).

The earlier picture by William Blake (figure 2) portrays the crucifixion of Christ.[19] It displays in vivid detail the vision of Jesus that Bunyan describes in the looking glass—the crown, the nails, the wounds, the spectacle, the mockery, the rejection. Neither the powers that crucify him nor the spectators who watch know that this man is "God's wisdom, secret and hidden, which God decreed before the ages for our glory . . . for if they had, they would not have crucified the Lord of glory" (1 Cor 2:7–8). Two figures stand out in the crowd. John, the beloved disciple, alone looks to the cross. The artist captures his fixed gaze, uplifted hands, and expression of wonder. Next to him is Mary, the mother of Jesus, whose head, though raised, cannot seem to look in the direction of her crucified son. The face of Christ is turned slightly in their direction. They love and trust him. They hear and obey him. They remain with him to the end, when he will say to them, "Woman, here is your son" and "Here is your mother" (John 19:26–27). The scene enables us to be grasped by the mystery that the Jesus we encounter in the written Word is not simply the man Jesus. It is Jesus who is identical with the eternal Word.

On May 29–31, 1934, a Confessional Synod of the German Evangelical Church met in Barmen, a city in northwestern Germany. There they adopted a statement with the title "Theological Declaration Concerning the Present Situation of the German Evangelical Church." The "present situation" the document refers to was the rise of national socialism and the struggle for control of the German Church. After Adolf Hitler became chancellor in January 1933, the German Christians aligned themselves with Nazi politics. In April 1933, the Nazi regime passed the so-called Aryan laws that excluded "non-Aryans" from civil service. The German Christians pressed for implementing an Aryan law within the churches and called for the dismissal of ministers and other church workers with Jewish ancestry. Churches displayed the German Christian banner with the swastika overlaying the cross. German Christians referred to Adolf Hitler as the messiah of the German people, and churches incorporated nationalist language into their worship. In the context of this Nazification of the German Church and culture, the Confessing Church was born.[20] The first thesis of the Barmen Declaration states, "Jesus Christ, as he is attested for us in Holy Scripture, is the one word of God which we have to hear and which we have to trust and obey in life and in death." It continues, "We reject the false doctrine, as though the Church could and would have to acknowledge as a source of its proclamation, apart from and besides this one Word of God, still other events and powers, figures and truths, as God's revelation."[21]

The substance of this declaration is as true now as it was then. Jesus Christ is the one Word of God. His incarnate faithfulness makes it possible for us to be his followers. He alone is "the objective possibility of our salvation."[22] As the letter to the Hebrews begins, "Long ago God spoke to our ancestors in many and various ways by the prophets, but in these last days he has spoken to us by a Son, whom he appointed heir of all things, through whom he also created the worlds" (Heb 1:1–2). Jesus Christ is the "one and the same Son," the eternal word of God. May we listen, trust, and obey.

Yours in Christ,

Interpreter

Figure 3

They came to a place at which a man is apt to lose his Way. Now, tho when it was light, their Guide could well enough tell how to miss those ways that led wrong, yet in the dark he was put to a stand: But he had in his Pocket a Map of all ways leading to, or from the Celestial City; wherefore he strook a Light (for he never goes also without his Tinder-box) and takes a view of his Book or Map; which bids him be careful in that place to turn to the right-hand-way. . . . Then thought I with my self, who, that goeth on Pilgrimage, but would have one of these Maps about him, that he may look when he is at a stand which is the way he must take?[1]

Mystery 2

Two Testaments: Christian Scripture

Dear Pilgrim:

I begin this letter with a simple question: What is the Bible? It seems to have an easy answer. At the desk where I am sitting, there is a black leather-bound book with the words *Holy Bible* embossed in gold letters on the cover. The contents page lists the names and order of the books: the Old Testament with thirty-nine and the New Testament with twenty-seven. The first part is about three times larger than the second. Next to it is another Bible that, unlike the first, opens right to left. On the cover, it has the title *TANAKH*, which is an acronym of the first Hebrew letter in its three divisions: Torah (Law), Nevi'im (Prophets), and Ketuvim (Writings). The first Bible is Protestant Christian, and the second is Jewish. The Protestant Christian Old Testament looks very similar to the Jewish Bible. They share a common set of books, but the Old Testament without the New Testament is neither a Jewish Bible nor a Christian one.[2] Though the Jewish and Christian Bibles contain many of the same texts, Jews and Christians read them quite differently. This difference is due to the Christian belief that the God of the New Testament, whom Jesus calls Abba or Father, is the God of Israel. It is a contested conviction between Christians and Jews, but we Christians cannot escape the struggle if we expect to give our story a truthful telling.[3] So let me offer a preliminary answer to my question. The Bible is comprised of two parts, the Old and New Testaments. Together they form one canon of Christian Scripture that bears a coherent witness to the God of Israel, who acted decisively for the salvation of the world in Jesus Christ.[4]

As I said to you in a previous letter, the Bible is the written Word that bears witness to the living Word. We pay attention to it, not simply because it is a record of what God has said but because we believe God continues to speak to us in it. As the sixteenth-century Swiss Protestant pastor and theologian Heinrich Bullinger put it, "God himself spoke to the fathers, prophets, apostles, and still speaks to us through the Holy Scriptures."[5] Some of us may have first heard that by singing the hymn:

> Jesus loves me, this I know,
> For the Bible tells me so.[6]

The Westminster Shorter Catechism taught generations of children to listen to God speaking in the Bible. It states, "The Word of God, which is contained in the Scriptures of the Old and New Testaments, is the only rule to direct us how we may glorify and enjoy [God],"[7] which is, as the catechism affirms in its very first question, the main purpose of our lives. Many others learned it in vacation Bible school by reciting together, "I pledge allegiance to the Bible, God's Holy Word, and will make it a lamp unto my feet, a light unto my path, and hide its words in my heart that I may not sin against God."[8] Through these and many other tradition-conveying practices, Christians have passed on the wisdom that the Bible is a guide for the pilgrim journey. The Bible is not simply a source for knowing about God. It teaches us to know God. More specifically, it teaches us to know God by its witness to the God of Israel, who acted for the salvation of the world in Jesus Christ.

In *The Pilgrim's Progress,* Bunyan shows us the importance of listening to God speak through the Bible.[9] The story opens with a burdened man, whose name is Christian, holding a book in his hands. As he reads, he cries out in distress, "What shall I do to be saved?" When Evangelist asks him why he is crying, Christian says the book has shown him that death and judgment await.[10] The book continues, warning him "to flee from the wrath to come" (Matt 3:7 KJV), and so he leaves his home and family to begin his pilgrim journey. Christian continues with the Bible as his guide until he crosses the River of Death and enters the Celestial City.[11]

Attending to the Bible is also a central theme of the second part of *The Pilgrim's Progress.* At House Beautiful, Prudence instructs the sons of Christiana to "be much in the Meditation of that Book that was the cause of your Father's becoming a Pilgrim."[12] At the Inn of Gaius, they gather in the morning before breakfast to read and discuss the Bible in family devotion.[13] Near the end of the story, Bunyan offers a series of figurative descriptions of the Bible. In our last letter, we examined his metaphor of the Bible as a looking glass, which from one perspective reflects a true image of the person who gazes into it but from another viewpoint presents the likeness of Christ.[14] Bunyan also describes the Bible as a sword that (citing Hebrews 4:12) "will cut Flesh, and Bones, and Soul, and Spirit,"[15] as well as a lantern that guides the pilgrims through the darkness at the end of their journey.[16] In the inscription above, Bunyan presents the Bible as a book or map that shows pilgrims all the ways to the Celestial City.[17] Without it, they would have no chance of making it to the end of their journey. Bunyan himself understood well the importance of listening to the Bible. He spent twelve years of his pilgrim journey in Bedford jail separated from his wife and children and the church community that he watched over and that nurtured him. During that dark time, God spoke to him through the Bible, giving him encouragement and strength to endure hopefully and to suffer joyfully.[18]

The earliest Christians, however, did not have the same two-part Bible that Bunyan had or that we have today. Their Scriptures were a collection of texts retained from Judaism. When the apostle Paul came to Thessalonica in northern Greece, he went to the Jewish synagogue on the Sabbath, where he "argued from the scriptures, explaining and proving that it was necessary for the Messiah to suffer and to rise from the dead, and saying, 'This is the Messiah, Jesus whom I am proclaiming to you'" (Acts 17:2–3). The sermon created an uproar in the city. Soon a crowd gathered at the house where Paul and his companions were staying. They shouted, "These people who have been turning the world upside down have come here also" (Acts 17:6). They accused them of violating "the decrees of the emperor, saying that there is another king named Jesus" (Acts 17:7). Realizing it was too dangerous to remain in Thessalonica, Paul and his fellow Christians went to the nearby town of Berea. There again, they went to the Jewish synagogue. The Bereans, however, "were more receptive than those in Thessalonica, for they welcomed the message very eagerly and examined the scriptures every day to see whether these things were so" (Acts 17:11). The "Scriptures" that Christians and Jews were reading in Thessalonica and Berea were the translation of the Hebrew Bible into Greek. The name of this Bible was the Septuagint. At the time, it was almost the "Authorized Version" of the Bible for Greek-speaking Jews and Christians.[19] Although the shape of their Bibles was different from now, Christians and Jews shared a common set of texts as Scripture. Yet the difference between them about how to read those texts remains a matter of much disagreement. For that reason alone, it is crucial for Christians and Jews to remain engaged in scriptural reasoning together "to see whether these things were so" (Acts 17:11) and whether they must remain so.

Gradually, Christians produced their own texts that they recognized as scriptural, and they gathered them into a literary body. The first collection was the letters of Paul, followed by the four Gospels. By 200 CE, the books of the New Testament were widely recognized as Christian Scripture. But to say the church recognized the Christian canon does not mean the church created its own Scripture. No official council determined the canon of Christian Scripture. Instead, Christians received these texts as canonical because they recognized God speaking in and through them. The authority of these books was not superimposed by the church. Rather, these books imposed themselves on the church. The church did not create its Scripture. The Word to which these books attest created the church. That the church recognized the canon authenticates the church as the church.[20] Christians accepted these texts as Scripture because they were true to the apostolic teaching that told the story of the God of Israel centered on Jesus Christ. There were some, like the second-century heretic Marcion, who argued for fewer books in the Christian canon, just as there were others, like the followers of the second-century prophet Montanus, who contended for a more open canon. Yet it is important to note that in recognizing the texts of the New Testament as Scripture, Christians continued to identify the Old Testament as Scripture. They believed God speaks in both testaments. Biblical scholar Brevard Childs summarizes the connection of the two parts well:

> The Christian canon consists of two different, separate voices, indeed of two different choirs of voices. The Old Testament is the voice of Israel, the New that of the

church. But beyond this, the voice of the New Testament
is largely that of a transformed Old Testament which is
now understood in the light of the gospel.[21]

Having a canon of Scripture does not say that these are the
only books Christians can read. Instead, it commends all of
these books as Scripture to be the rule and guide for reading,
hearing, and discerning the Word of God.

You still may be wondering why these two parts are called
testaments. The English word comes from the Latin *testamen-
tum*, which, like the Greek word *diatheke* that it translates,
means "testament" or "covenant." This is the sense when it
names the two parts of the Christian canon. When Jesus celebrated the Last Supper with his disciples, he described the
meal they shared as an enactment of "the new covenant" made
through his death (1 Cor 11:25; Mark 14:24; Luke 22:20; also
Heb 9:15). The new covenant enables Christians to participate
in the covenant promise God made to Abraham that "all the
Gentiles shall be blessed in you" (Gal 3:8). Christ is the offspring of Abraham (Gal 3:17) and the heir to the promise of
the covenant that "in you all the families of the earth shall be
blessed" (Gen 12:3). Those who have been baptized into Christ
are then children of God, and because they belong to Christ,
the heir of the covenant promise, they are also children of
Abraham and heirs to the covenant promise (Gal 3:26–29).[22]
The new covenant, however, does not abolish the old covenant.
For God promised Abraham, "I will establish my covenant
between me and you, and your offspring after you throughout
their generations, for an everlasting covenant, to be God to you
and to your offspring after you" (Gen 17:7). Some Christians
have concluded that because the children of Abraham have not
accepted Jesus as the Messiah, the old covenant is no longer
binding, but God declared that the covenant was everlasting.
How do we make sense of this? The apostle Paul provides

some help. He explains that despite Israel's unbelief, "God has not rejected his people" (Rom 11:2). Rather, Gentile followers of Christ have been grafted into God's covenant with Israel. This means Gentiles and Jews are now one people of God, but the reality of their unity is a "mystery" not yet revealed (Rom 11:25). Israel's rejection of Christ, Paul states, is only temporary. After the full number of Gentiles enters the people of God and shares in the promise, "all Israel will be saved" (Rom 11:25). He does not seek to explain the mystery still hidden. Instead, he cautions that because God's judgments are "unsearchable" and God's ways are "inscrutable" (Rom 11:33), we must be patient and trust in God's faithfulness. "For," he asks, "who has known the mind of the Lord?" (Rom 11:34)

In a previous letter, I mentioned the German Christians who made their church teaching and practice conform to the politics of the Nazis. The German Baptists did not follow the National Church, but they also did not support the Confessing Church. Instead, the official position of the Union remained impartial and nonpolitical, supporting neither. They told themselves that their middle-of-the-road stance gave them the freedom to preach the gospel. In truth, it caused them to ignore the suffering of the Jews under Hitler.[23] Until recently, the official confessional statement for the Swiss, Austrian, and two German Baptist Unions read, "The new covenant, in which God has established his rule of grace for all men, *dissolves the old covenant* and at the same time brings it to fulfillment."[24] These words reflect a supersessionist view in which the church has replaced Israel as the people of God. A recent revision of the confession rejects supersessionism and affirms that God's covenant with Israel has never been revoked or replaced, and therefore Christians must acknowledge God's everlasting covenant with God's people, the Jews. The revised statement emphatically declares, "*God has not dissolved his covenant with Israel* when he founded a new covenant through

Jesus Christ and thereupon established his reign of grace for all people."[25] The German Baptist Union established a special Committee on Christian-Jewish Relations, which drafted the revised statement. Since 2007, the Union has urged congregations to observe a special "Israel Sunday" and a remembrance of our shared history. Examples like these are signs of Christians doing the hard work of staying in conversation with their elder brothers and sisters, the Jews.

Yet many, like the second-century Christian philosopher Justin Martyr, have maintained that the new covenant superseded the old covenant and that Gentile Christians are the true people of Israel.[26] There are passages in the Bible that may seem to suggest a basis for supersessionism. The theology that the church has displaced Israel in the history of salvation has been widely held throughout history, but important theological voices have begun to question it.[27] As one theologian has noted, Israel and the church belong together:

> The Church's story understood as continuous with Israel's, tells of God doing in this time between the times what he has done before: choosing and guiding a people to be a sign and witness in all that it is and does, whether obediently or disobediently, to who and what he is. Both God's mercy and God's judgment are manifest in the life of this people as nowhere else.[28]

Holding the mystery that these two testaments tell the story of the one people of God, however, is not easy. It may be tempting for Christians simply to focus their attention on the New Testament, but these books only rightly find their place following after and read with the Old Testament. Together, the Old and New Testaments form the one canon of Christian Scripture. Saint Augustine summarized it this way: the New Testament is concealed in the Old, and the Old Testament is revealed in the New.[29] This is true, but even more importantly, the two testaments find their place in the one canon of Scripture because both attest to the same subject—Jesus Christ, the one Word of God. The Old Testament looks forward to a Messiah who is to come. The New Testament looks back on a Messiah who has already come. The first is a witness of expectation. The second is a witness of recollection. Like Blake's painting of the two angels watching over the body of Christ in the sepulcher (figure 3),[30] the Old and New Testaments lean toward each other as they lean toward Christ. The diversity of the sacred texts does not find a unity in any theological system or interpretive scheme that we may apply to them. The two testaments in the canon of Christian Scripture are one because the subject to whom they witness, Jesus Christ, is one.[31] If that is true, discerning this mystery will take a lifetime and maybe longer.

Yours under the Word,

Interpreter

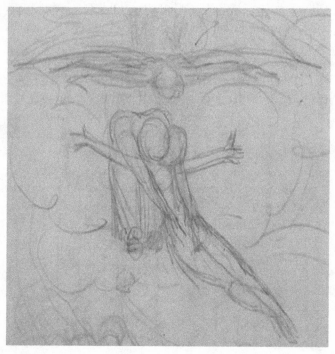

Figure 4

Prudence: Canst thou tell who made thee?
James: God the Father, God the Son, and God the Holy Ghost.
Prudence: And canst thou tell who saves thee?
James: God the Father, God the Son, and God the Holy Ghost.[1]

Mystery 3

Three Persons: The Holy Trinity

DEAR PILGRIM:

There is a story of a preacher who, after reading a rather cryptic passage from the Scripture, took off his spectacles, closed the Bible, and announced, "Brothers and sisters, this morning I intend to explain the unexplainable, find out the undefinable, ponder over the imponderable, and unscrew the inscrutable."[2] For more than a few Christians, the mystery of the Trinity could do with a little "unscrewing." We confess our faith in God's three-in-oneness and punctuate it in doxology to "Father, Son, and Holy Ghost." Yet I suspect we are often just confused. One of my favorite examples of theological confusion about the Trinity is a scene from the movie *Nuns on the Run*, when Sister Inviolata of the Immaculate Conception "explains" the Trinity to Sister Euphemia of the Five Wounds. After Sister Inviolata's explanation, Sister Euphemia summarizes what she has heard: "God is his Son, and his Son is God, but his Son moonlights as a Holy Ghost, a Holy Spirit, and a dove, and they all sent each other even though they are one in the same thing." When Sister Inviolata tells her she has it, Sister Euphemia asks, "Wait a minute! Does that make any sense to you?" To which Sister Inviolata replies, "No, and it

makes no sense to anybody. That's why you have to believe it."[3]
This way of thinking follows the old theological adage that
warns that if you try to understand the Trinity, you will
lose your mind, but if you deny it, you will lose your soul.[4]
The Trinity consequently remains for many Christians an
arcane doctrine they must believe despite its seeming lack of
theological coherence or practical relevance. I hope you might
begin to see this language of God's three-in-oneness as a way
of talking that helps make some sense of what we are saying
about the mystery of God's love revealed in Jesus Christ that
through the Holy Spirit gives life to the world.

First, the Trinity is a way for Christians to speak about
One who is greater than our utmost imagination, nearer than
our inmost thoughts, and realer than our own existence. The
Trinity is about mystery, not math. In the statement that there
are three persons in the Holy Trinity, three is not a number
because if it is a number, it becomes impossible to display the
relationship among the three persons. Moreover, the word *person* in the language of the creed does not mean what we mean
by *person* today. The three persons of the Trinity are not three
distinct subjective centers of consciousness who think and act
independently of one another. God has three ways of being
God that think and act together. These three are one. To paraphrase a line from Saint Augustine in his treatise *On the Trinity*,
when we say that God is one and three, we do not mean that
God is one thing and three things, but we say something so
that we do not say nothing.[5]

There is a legendary story about Augustine walking along
the beach to clear his mind as he was writing his book *On
the Trinity*. On the way, he saw a child who was scooping
water from the sea with a spoon and pouring it into a small
hole he had dug in the sand. When Augustine asked what he
was doing, the child replied, "I am emptying the sea into this

little hole of mine." Augustine exclaimed, "That is impossible, for the sea is so great, and your spoon is so small." The child answered, "Yes, but I shall sooner draw all the water of the sea into this hole than you will bring the mystery of the Trinity into human understanding."[6] As the Scripture says, "Out of the mouth of babes" (Ps 8:2).

To say the one God has three ways of being at the same time confronts us with the deep mystery of God's inner life that transcends our conceptual capacities. It is a way of saying the God who is eternal and exists before all things is the same God who loved the world by sending God's own Son (John 3:16) and gives life to the world through God's Holy Spirit (John 3:6–8). That is why all those analogies about God being like an apple with skin, fruit, and core, or an egg with shell, white, and yolk, or even a shamrock with three leaves in one plant always end up confusing us and making the problem worse. God is not three but one who has three ways of being God. Believing in the triune God is not a matter of getting our arithmetic right. It is a way of speaking about the mystery of God's very being.

Second, the Trinity gives Christians language that addresses the relational and personal reality of God. There are challenges, to be sure, in using this received language. Some theologians have argued that the terms *Father, Son,* and *Spirit*, although appropriate in the Greco-Roman culture that was patriarchal, are inappropriate today. They urge us to consider "how we might name and praise God in counterpatriarchal ways more faithful to the Christian gospel."[7] One way to expand our God-language is to retrieve feminine images for God in the Bible like mother (Isa 49:15), midwife (Ps 17:8), and wisdom (Prov 8:23–25). Another possibility is to use synthetic biblical images that describe the Son as begotten (John 1:18) and the Spirit as proceeding (John 20:21–22) from a

Motherly-Father.[8] These important critiques offer constructive steps in our language about God. Using male and female
images for God with equivalency can have a subversive effect
on patriarchal theologies and practices in the church.[9] However, some have argued that equivalency in gendered images of
God does not go far enough. They have advocated for substi-
tuting nongender-specific terms like Creator, Redeemer, and
Sanctifier in the place of Father, Son, and Spirit to get around
the confusion that traditional language might be mistaken as
ascribing male gender to God.

At first glance, there may seem to be nothing wrong with
nongender-specific language. God is surely due praise for the
acts of creation, redemption, and sanctification, and patriarchal language for God has been used to justify the subor-
dination of women in the church. However, these substitute
terms are not adequate replacements for the historic formu-
lations. Much of the new proposed language describes *actions*
of the triune God. These actions do not name the *persons* of
the Trinity nor the *relations* among the persons. More importantly, none of these actions is the work of one divine person
acting alone. All three persons of the Trinity participate in
the creating, redeeming, and sanctifying of the world.[10] The
result of a well-intentioned revisionism has the unhappy consequence of reviving the ancient heresy of modalism, where
the one God has three successive modes of being.[11] Despite
the challenges, it would seem that Christians are better off
retaining the received language of the Trinity because it con-
veys the relational and personal dimension of God. Yet the
question that remains is whether it is possible to conserve the
received language while also attending to the problems of gender exclusiveness.

In 1982, the ministers of the Riverside Church in New
York City started using a gender-inclusive formula for baptism,

in which they baptized in the name of "God the Creator, Christ the Redeemer, and the Holy Spirit our Constant Companion." James F. Kay, then a doctoral student and tutor in systematic theology, wrote the ministers, stating that the new gender-inclusive formula was not trinitarian. He proposed as an alternative that they baptize "in the name of the Father, and of the Son, and of the Holy Spirit—our Mother." Kay's theological reasoning drew from the fourteenth-century English anchoress Julian of Norwich, who identified the mothering activity and office of all three divine persons, as well as feminine allusions and images of God in the Bible (e.g., Deut 32:18; Isa 49:14–16, 66:13; Hosea 11:3–4; Matt 23:37; and Luke 13:37). The pastors agreed with Kay's critique and proposal, although they slightly amended his formulation to "in the name of the Father and of the Son and of the Holy Spirit, One God, Mother of us all."[12] The expanded trinitarian formula continues to be popular among those who seek to retain the received ancient ecumenical grammar while accommodating contemporary critiques of gender-exclusive language. The addition of the gender-expansive appendix "One God, Mother of us all," however, has yet to gain widespread use in Christian liturgy and worship.[13]

I recently read a statement by a scholar who described the Trinity as a "mangled metaphor." It was an attempt to be clever, but it badly missed the point. A metaphor is a figure of speech that enables us to "speak about one thing in terms which are seen to be suggestive of another."[14] The Trinity uses metaphorical language, but it is not merely an extended metaphor. To speak of God as Father, Son, and Spirit implies a stretching of these terms so that our language of the persons in the Trinity is more analogical than metaphorical. As Augustine suggested, it enables us *to say something* so that we are not left *to say nothing*. When Christians speak of God as

Father, they are not just saying, "God is like a Father." God is certainly like a father, and a mother for that matter, but *Father* in trinitarian language is not just suggesting an analogy for God. It names the God of Jesus Christ, who he called his Abba-Father (John 17:1) and who he invited us to call our Abba-Father (Matt 6:9). It is the Spirit who confirms that we are children of God when we cry, "Abba Father" (Rom 8:15). This historic language of Father, Son, and Spirit is crucial because it expresses the relations within the life of the triune God. The Father is Father because the Father has a Son, and the Son is Son because the Son has a Father, and the Spirit is Spirit because of the love shared between Father and Son. The Father names the Son (Mark 1:11; Matt 3:17), and the Son names the Father (Matt 26:39), and the Father and Son name their Spirit (John 15:26; 20:21–22).[15] These three—Father, Son, and Holy Spirit—together as one are not just a metaphor or an analogy for God. The Trinity is the divine name, and the reception of God's name comes by revelation. God declared to Moses, "I appeared to Abraham, Isaac, and Jacob as God Almighty, but *by my name* 'The Lord' I did not make myself known to them" (Exod 6:3). God explains that the purpose of this self-disclosure to Israel was to make God's "name resound through all the earth" (Exod 9:16). The Trinity—the Father, Son, and Holy Spirit—is the name of God revealed to the church (Matt 28:19), just as the "I Am" is the name of God revealed to Israel (Exod 3:14). It is no surprise, then, that Jesus commands his followers to make disciples and baptize them *in the name* (not the names) of the Father and of the Son and of the Holy Spirit and to extend the name to the end of the age (Matt 28:20).

Third, the language of the Trinity offers a theological grammar that enables us to talk *about* and *to* God. As the Jewish theologian Martin Buber wrote, the "names of God remain hallowed—because they have been used not only to speak *of* God, but also to speak *to* him."[16] Yet we must know what to say as well as what not to say. One of the great theologians of the Christian faith, Athanasius of Alexandria, who helped shape the reception of the Nicene Creed, put it very simply: Whatever we say about the Father, we also say about the Son and the Spirit, except the Son and Spirit are not the Father.[17] All three persons are God, yet the three are distinct from one another. A diagram, sometimes called the shield of faith, has visually represented this theological grammar. It has one node at each point of the triangle, one for each person of the Trinity. At the center of the triangle is another node with the word *God*. Each of the outer nodes connects to the center node with the word *is*. Each of the outer nodes connects to one another with the words *is not*. The result is a simple grammatical formulation: the Father is God, the Son is God, the Holy Spirit is God, and the Father is not the Son, the Son is not the Holy Spirit, and the Holy Spirit is not the Father. This trinitarian grammar gives us basic rules for talking about God's life in the world. Because we have this language, we can read all of Scripture as the unfolding narrative of the triune God. It guides our speech with simplicity and clarity; as fourth-century theologian Gregory of Nazianzus explained, when we say "God," we mean "the Trinity—Father, Son, and Holy Spirit."[18]

Without the theological grammar provided by the doctrine of the Trinity, we would remain as confused as Nicodemus trying to sort out what is going on in Jesus. His confusion is understandable. As a Jew, Nicodemus was a monotheist who believed the most basic conviction of the faith of Israel: "Hear, O Israel: The Lord is our God, the Lord alone" (Deut 6:4). It may also be translated as "The Lord our God is one Lord" (Deut 6:4, KJV). But if the Lord is one, how can Christians confess that Jesus is Lord (Rom 10:9–10)? How can Christians pray to Jesus (1 Cor 16:22) and also pray to the Father (Matt

6:9)? These claims seem incompatible. "What is going on here?" modern monotheists rightly ask with Nicodemus. His best guess was that Jesus was a teacher sent by God; otherwise, how could he perform miraculous signs (John 3:2)? Thomas Jefferson also believed in both a creative and personal God and that Jesus was a great moral teacher, although he did not think Jesus performed miracles, which he thought violated the laws of nature.[19] Nicodemus and Jefferson were partly right. Jesus was a teacher, but he was more than just a teacher.

Several years ago, I made the provocative statement that "most Baptists are Unitarians that simply have not gotten around to denying the Trinity."[20] I was not suggesting that my fellow Baptists were deists like Thomas Jefferson, who refused to believe in the Trinity. Nevertheless, I perceived a widespread functional Unitarianism that lay just beneath the surface of our professed orthodoxy. The piety of evangelicals tilts toward a Unitarianism of the Second Person, just as for progressives it leans in the direction of a Unitarianism of the First Person.[21] The comment was not well received. Some time later, I got a note from a friend, who had initially resisted my remark. He brought to my attention a survey of evangelical Christians in the United States. Among the findings, one fifth claimed that Jesus was the first creature created by God, and more than half said that the Holy Spirit is an impersonal force rather than a personal being.[22] It was no consolation to be confirmed in my worry.

In his wonderful little book *Worship, Community, and the Triune God*, Scottish theologian James Torrance suggested that most Christians are likewise confused. We go to church, sing our hymns, listen to the sermon, pray for the world, and present our offerings to God. We recognize we need God's grace to do it, and we have a good example in Jesus to show us how, but we think of worship as what *we* do before God. What this suggests, Torrance says, is that the only priesthood is *our* priesthood, the only offering is *our* offering, and the only intercession is *our* intercession. However, this description of worship, Torrance warns, is *Unitarian*. It has no need of Christ as mediator; it is human-centered and has no place for the Spirit because we can handle it.[23] Torrance points out that *trinitarian* faith offers a rich resource to describe what is going on in worship, where we participate through the Spirit in the incarnate Son's communion with the Father.[24] To put it simply, the Trinity is God's love language for the world. Through Word and Spirit, we participate with the triune God in the drama of the world's redemption. In this divine work, Christ alone is the Mediator between God and humanity, and the Holy Spirit is the life-giving love that animates our faith and enables us to participate through baptism in union with Christ's death and to be reborn into new life (John 3:3–8; Rom 6:4).

Here is the good news: You do not have to understand it. Nicodemus did not understand it, and neither do we, and yet we believe. We believe in the Trinity even though we do not fully understand the mystery of God's love. As the Scripture says, "We walk by faith, not by sight" (2 Cor 5:7). We do not seek to understand in order to believe. We believe that we might understand. For, as Augustine put it, "unless you believe, you shall not understand."[25] Faith simply opens the door of possibility for understanding. The doctrine of the Trinity in itself does not make complete sense, but when by faith we confess God's three-in-oneness, we move toward an understanding of other things.

The inscription above from *The Pilgrim's Progress* comes when Christiana and her four sons arrive at House Beautiful, which is a representation of the gathered church. Upon arrival, the community receives the visitors into their fellowship and welcomes them to the table for the breaking of bread as they did their father, Christian. After evening prayers, they retire to their chamber for the evening. The next day, one of the members, Prudence, offers to catechize the boys, who have been baptized but not yet instructed in the teaching of Christ or the mystery of the gospel. She begins with the youngest, James. She asks the catechetical questions: Who made you? Who saves you? He answers: God made me, and God saves me. For God alone is Creator and Savior, but his response says more. The triune God creates and saves. Yet it is not the Father who is Creator and Christ who is the Savior. God the Father, God the Son, and God the Holy Spirit makes and saves. The Holy Trinity, one God in three Persons, is Creator and Savior. James has answered well.

The drawing by William Blake (figure 4) attempts to show visually what young James has affirmed.[26] The Father, who is not noticeably male, embraces the Son, who is not noticeably male either. The Father's embrace supports the Son's visibly outstretched arms on an invisible cross. The noticeably non-gendered Spirit majestically hovers above with wings extended as a reflection of the Son's outstretched arms and the Father's embrace, gently sheltering the Father, who embraces the Son, and the Son, who rests in the Father.[27] It resonates with the words of the Psalmist:

> You who live in the shelter of the Most High,
>   who abide in the shadow of the Almighty,
> will say to the Lord, "My refuge and my fortress;
>   my God, in whom I trust."
> For he will deliver you from the snare of the fowler
>   and from the deadly pestilence;
> he will cover you with his pinions,
>   and under his wings you will find refuge.
>   (Ps 91:1–4)

The Father, the Son, and the Spirit—the three-in-one God—is the life-giving gift that is the mystery of love for the whole world. One triune God: almighty Creator, vulnerable Savior, life-giving Presence. So we pray,

> Lord Jesus Christ, who didst stretch out thine arms of love on the hard wood of the cross that everyone might come within the reach of thy saving embrace: So clothe us in thy Spirit that we, reaching forth our hands in love, may bring those who do not know thee to the knowledge and love of thee; for the honor of thy Name.[28]

> Yours in the name of the Father, the Son, and the Holy Spirit, One God, Mother of us all,
> *Interpreter*

Figure 5

Prudence: What do you think of the Bible?
Matthew: It is the Holy word of God.
Prudence: Is there nothing Written therein, but what you understand?
Matthew: Yes, a great deal.
Prudence: What do you do when you meet with such places therein, that you do not understand?
Matthew: I think God is wiser than I. I pray also that he will please to let me know all therein that he knows will be for my good.[1]

Mystery 4

Four Senses: Reading Literally and Spiritually

DEAR PILGRIM:

The theme of these letters is the mystery of the gospel "that was kept secret for long ages but is now disclosed, and through the prophetic writings is made known to all" (Rom 16:25–26). The Bible is both the record and revelation of that mystery. The promise that Jesus made to his disciples, he makes to all who follow him: "To you it has been given to know the mysteries" (Matt 13:11). Yet discerning the mystery in the Scriptures is not as simple as reading your daily newsfeed. As Jesus told his followers, "If you continue in my word, you are truly my disciples; and you will know the truth, and the truth will make you free" (John 8:31–32). This statement raises the question about what it means to continue in the Word or, to put it differently, how to read Christian Scripture. God continues to speak to us in and through it because Scripture is inspired (2 Tim 3:16). To say that it is inspired does not simply mean that when we read the Bible, it has an uplifting effect on us. To affirm that Scripture is inspired means we sense that these books are truly "God-breathed." Human authors and editors had a hand in writing and collecting the books, yet the inspiration of Scripture means more. We turn to these books with the conviction that "no prophecy ever came by human will, but men and women moved by the Holy Spirit spoke from God" (2 Pet 1:21). This means the ultimate author of Holy Scripture is the triune God, who inspired the human authors to write and who continues to speak through the words they wrote.[2]

I confess that when I began to take seriously Christ's admonition to continue in the Word, I found it to be a challenge. It did not seem that God was always speaking to me in all parts of the Bible. Nevertheless, I struggled to be a more faithful reader. I think my approach then was limited to seeking the "plain meaning" or the "literal sense" of Scripture.[3] That was until I heard a sermon by a preacher, who was editor of our state denominational newspaper. He began with the declaration, "Salvation through Jesus Christ is the theme of every book in the Bible."[4] He then proceeded to show us from Genesis to Revelation. It was a stunning performance of rhetoric, but it left me wondering how he had found Jesus, especially in those obscure Old Testament books. Our pastor told me these "other meanings" lie hidden beneath the literal and could be found only by spiritualizing the text, which he discouraged. Not long after that, I went off to university, where I studied the Bible and biblical languages. I grew suspicious of spiritualizing or allegory that diverted attention away from the plain, literal, grammatical, historical sense of the text. I came to believe that *the meaning* of a biblical text was identical with its *historical reference*. As one scholar succinctly put it, the primary task of biblical interpretation is to determine *what it meant*, not *what it means*.[5]

When I became a pastor charged with preaching from the Bible Sunday after Sunday, it became harder to maintain this distinction between *meant* and *means*. I realized the congregation did not gather to hear me give a history lesson. They came expecting to receive a word from God in my sermon.

The difficulty reached a crisis as I prepared to preach one Sunday from Isaiah 53. I realized that if I only attended to what the prophet Isaiah meant, I would have little to say about what it means to us. Even more troubling, I knew I had no sense of how to connect the Suffering Servant of Isaiah 53 with Jesus of Nazareth, which Christian preaching had done since the sermon of Philip to the Ethiopian on the road from Jerusalem to Gaza (Acts 8:26–40). It was a turning point in my thinking. As I read the Bible with new eyes, I began to see that the earliest Christians read the Old Testament very differently than I thought. For example, when the apostle Paul referred to how the Israelites got water from a rock in the desert (Exod 17:6; Num 20:10–11), he said, "They drank from the spiritual rock that followed them, and the rock was Christ" (1 Cor 10:4). He did not say the rock pointed to or was a prophecy about Christ. He said the rock *was* Christ. Moreover, Christ did not only appear those two times in the wilderness. Paul says Christ traveled with them throughout their forty-year journey. This shocking metaphor is an example of what New Testament scholar Richard Hays describes as *reading backwards*.[6] The apostle Paul was not alone in reading this way. Each of the four Gospels shows how Israel's Scripture mysteriously prefigures Jesus. The fourth Gospel puts it concisely: "If you believed Moses, you would believe me, for he wrote about me" (John 5:46).

This imaginative way of reading the Bible did not stop with the apostles. Post-apostolic Christian readers recognized that since the Scriptures were spiritual writings, literal meanings alone were insufficient to understand their fuller sense. They realized that the Scriptures must also be read spiritually. As a basis for this conviction, they often pointed to the words of the apostle Paul: "The letter kills, but the Spirit gives life" (2 Cor 3:6). They approached the Scriptures with the belief that the deep mystery hidden within these books could only be discerned through spiritual interpretation. As Jerome, the late-fourth-century Christian scholar, declared upon reading a passage from the Gospel of Mark, "We shall inquire into the significance of the words in order to fathom the mystery contained in the text."[7] When properly instructed in the spiritual meaning of Scripture, Augustine of Hippo noted, the result is the formation of the virtues of faith, hope, and love.[8] As he cautioned, "Whoever . . . thinks that he understands the Holy Scriptures, or any part of them, but puts such an interpretation on them that does not tend to build up this twofold love of God and our neighbor, does not yet understand them as he ought."[9]

From the time of John Cassian in the early fifth century, the spiritual sense was subdivided into three categories: the allegorical sense that taught faith, the moral sense that instructed in the way of love, and the anagogical sense that pointed to future hope.[10] Nicholas of Lyra summarized the fourfold doctrine this way:

> The letter teaches what took place,
> The allegory what to believe,
> The moral what to do.
> The anagogy what goal to strive for.[11]

As the five basic human senses—touch, sight, hearing, smell, and taste—enable us to perceive what is going on in the world, the four senses of Scripture have guided Christians to discern the mystery of what God is doing in this world and the next.

Within the scheme of the fourfold method, the literal sense (used interchangeably with the historical sense) was explicitly regarded as the foundation of other meanings. As Henri de Lubac, the great scholar of the history of Christian biblical interpretation, put it, "The mystery follows the history."[12] The connection between the literal and spiritual is one of essential interdependency and dynamic continuity. Nevertheless, de Lubac admits that the practice of the spiritual interpretation seems to invite extravagant spiritualized speculation. The result is a flattening-out of the biblical narrative and the imposition of arbitrary meanings that pay little attention to the scope of the text or the underlying events of history. Martin Luther, John Calvin, and other Protestant Christians warned about what they regarded to be the extreme allegorizing of the Bible by earlier Christian interpreters. One of the often-cited examples of such allegorical abuse is Augustine's well-known interpretation of the parable of the Good Samaritan. Augustine ascribed meanings to every detail of the story, proposing that the man traveling from Jerusalem to Jericho is Adam, Jerusalem is the heavenly city, the thieves are the devil and his angels, the priest and the Levite are the Old Testament, the binding of the wounds are the restraint of sin, the oil is hope and the wine the Spirit, the inn is the church, the two denarii are the love of God and neighbor, the innkeeper is the apostle Paul, the promise to repay more is the counsel of celibacy, and the Samaritan is Christ.[13]

Commenting on Augustine's interpretation of the parable, the twentieth-century New Testament scholar C. H. Dodd conceded that the allegorical method has been widely practiced throughout history, but he suggested that "the ordinary person of intelligence" would find this kind of "mystification" of the story "quite perverse."[14] Dodd contended that the problem with allegorization is not simply that it is "overdone or fanciful." Instead, in his view, it goes against the nature and purpose of parables, which he argued are not *allegories* with multiple meanings intended for a Greek audience but *metaphors* having a single meaning addressed to Jewish listeners.[15] Dodd's thesis has held considerable influence over the interpretation of parables ever since. For all his criticism of allegory, in that book, Dodd never indicated how to interpret the parable historically. Focusing on the social context of the parable's original hearers as he recommended certainly draws attention to the surprising turn that a Samaritan, a historic enemy of the Jews, is the one who shows mercy. In doing so, it echoes the Old Testament story of the prophet Oded, who persuaded the Samaritans to help their Judean captives (2 Chr 28:8–15). As one New Testament scholar suggests, the parable of the Good Samaritan shows "that enemies can prove to be neighbors, that compassion has no boundaries, and that judging people on the basis of their religion or ethnicity will leave us dying in a ditch."[16]

However, the historical approach misses something that Augustine's allegorical rendering seems to get right with its central meaning that Jesus is the Samaritan. Where the historical method attends to discrete textual units separated from the larger literary whole, Augustine's christological stress places the parable in the gospel narrative and the larger canonical setting. In so doing, Augustine points to the way this parable shows the whole gospel story of the incarnate faithfulness of Jesus Christ. Augustine is not alone in this sort of allegorical reading or in the identification of the Samaritan with Christ. His interpretation follows similar lines to the homily on the parable by Origen of Alexandria.[17] It is a reminder that even though allegorical meanings can be arbitrary and disconnected from the literal/historical sense of biblical text, attending to the multiple senses of a passage can also serve to discern the deeper mystery hidden within the Scriptures.

Two French scholars, Henri de Lubac and Jean Danielou, have been especially influential by providing sophisticated accounts that have corrected misunderstandings and encouraged the recovery of "the spiritual understanding of the

Scriptures, as it existed during the Christian centuries."[18] De Lubac explains:

> The allegorical meaning was the dogmatic meaning par excellence, and it was firmly rooted in history. Far from compromising the historical foundations of the faith, it actually insured for all Christian thought the essentially historical character which is so perfectly in keeping with the Christian faith, but which has so often been disturbingly blurred.[19]

The allegorical and historical meanings, de Lubac continues, are distinct from but connected with one another.[20]

You might be wondering where that leaves us with the story I told at the beginning of this letter. The preacher's spiritualizing in that sermon was weak in that it attended very little to the literal-historical sense, but the assertion that Christ is the central theme of the Christian Scriptures is a crucial Christian conviction worth understanding. It is encouraging to see Christians approaching the Scriptures not as a *problem to solve* through the application of critical skills but as a *mystery to discern* by returning to the use of the literal and spiritual senses.[21] I do not expect that there will be a rush to embrace the classic doctrine of the fourfold method; however, I do favor a return to the spirit of it by exploring the fuller sense (*sensus plenior*) of the Scriptures.[22] To that end, I offer four rules as guides for readers who seek to discern the mystery of Christian Scripture.[23]

First, reading the Bible with an eye to this fuller sense appeals to *the help of the Spirit*. Rabbi and philosopher Abraham Heschel observed that "to be able to encounter the spirit within the words [of the Bible], we must learn to crave for an affinity with the pathos of God." He continued, "To sense the presence of God in the Bible, one must learn *to be present* to

God in the Bible."[24] In my earlier collection of letters, I urged you to continue in the Word through the practice of continuous reading, or *lectio continua*. I now commend you to engage the Bible through the practice of spiritual reading, or *lectio divina*. The Cistercian monk Arnoul of Boheriss described the practice of *lectio* in this way:

> When he reads, let him seek for savor, not science. The Holy Scripture is the well of Jacob from which the waters are drawn which will be poured out later in prayer. Thus there will be no need to go to the oratory to begin to pray; but in reading itself, means will be found for prayer and contemplation.[25]

Reading the Bible with the help of the Spirit is a matter of listening. There is not one meaning fixed for all time but multiple meanings that break forth anew each time we read. The Bible in this spiritual sense is not an object of study; rather, we as readers are the object as God, who is present in the Bible, speaks through the Spirit. I hope you will learn to read the Scriptures with the help of the Spirit of truth, our Advocate and Helper, who guides us in all truth (John 15:16–17).

Second, an openness to the fuller sense of Scripture is cultivated when our reading attends to *the remembrance of the Lord*. As we have seen above, allegory, especially christologically centered allegory, has often managed to stay connected with the gospel shape of biblical narrative in ways that historical critical interpretation has not. Yet we might ask how to pay closer attention to both the literal and spiritual senses when reading christologically. Consider, for example, the statement by the risen Christ to his disciples on the shore of the Sea of Galilee that "everything written about me in the law of Moses, the prophets, *and the psalms* must be fulfilled" (Luke 24:44). The Protestant theologian Dietrich Bonhoeffer pointed to the voice in the Psalter that protests his innocence, invokes God's judgment, and proclaims infinite suffering. This voice, Bonhoeffer says, is Jesus Christ, who prayed the prayers of the messianic king from whose line the promised Messiah would descend.[26] Bonhoeffer's christological reading follows a line of interpretation proposed by the apostle Paul, who also says the words of the Psalmist not only speak *about* Christ but are spoken *by* Christ. The apostle writes (quoting Psalm 69:9) that Christ declares, "The insults of those who insult you have fallen on me" (Rom 15:3). It points to the incarnate faithfulness of Christ as the model of imitation for Jews and Gentiles in the Church of Rome. The apostle adds that his Christian audience should study the Scriptures, later known as the Old Testament, "for whatever was written in former days was written for our instruction, so that by steadfastness and by the encouragement of the scriptures we might have hope" (Rom 15:4). Old Testament scholar Stephen Chapman offers a helpful comment about this line of interpretation:

> The speaking voice of the Psalms is christological not merely in predicting Christ, or even in foreshadowing Christ in a typological fashion, although Bonhoeffer affirms these aspects of the Psalter as well. The voice of the Psalter is christological above all for him in the sense of actually having been spoken by the Christ who was spiritually present "in" the David of history.[27]

Bonhoeffer provides a good example of reading the Bible by remembering Jesus with an eye to both the literal and spiritual sense of the text. When the christological rule guides our reading, our interpretive vision becomes open to the fuller sense of Scripture.

Third, what it means to read the Bible spiritually and christologically finds concrete human examples in *the imitation of*

the saints. The exemplary performances of holy people guide
our reading by showing us what Scripture looks like when we
live it out. As the apostle Paul said to the church in Corinth,
"Be imitators of me, as I am of Christ" (1 Cor 11:1). Historian Robert Wilken states that this mimetic process of holiness in early Christianity taught that the way to virtue was
"by observing the lives of holy men and women and imitating
their deeds."[28] I want to suggest further that the extent to
which Christians become good *Bible readers* correlates with
the habits they acquire by being careful *saint watchers*. You
may still wonder why we should imitate the lives of other
Christians, even very good ones. Catholic theologian Karl
Rahner offers an excellent answer. He says,

> Herein lies the special task which the canonized Saints
> have to fulfill for the Church. They are the initiator
> and the creative models of the holiness which happens
> to be right for, and is the task of, their particular age.
> They create a new style; they prove that a certain form
> of life and activity is a really genuine possibility; they
> show experimentally that one can be a Christian even
> in "this" way.[29]

Classic collections like Butler's *Lives of the Saints* (1756–1759)
arrange their stories around the liturgical calendar, and contemporary editions like Robert Ellsberg's *All Saints* feature
daily profiles of "Saints, Prophets, and Witnesses for Our
Time."[30] The lives of the saints visibly and tangibly represent
the life of Christ and invite imitation of the way of life displayed there as a faithful response of discipleship. Without
the saints, we would find it difficult to imagine what it might
mean to follow Jesus faithfully, but because we can trust their
lives to be truthful representations of Jesus, we can imitate
their exemplary performances of Scripture.

Fourth, our Bible reading is enriched when it is guided by *the discernment of the community*. This rule arises out of the conviction that "Scripture is addressed principally to communities constituted and reconstituted by the triune God," and therefore "Scripture itself calls for the formation and reformation of communities of people living faithfully before the God of Jesus Christ."[31] Reading in communion with other Christians encourages personal engagement with Scripture, but when we read in communion, individual interpretation "is always subject to 'congregational hermeneutics,' to the mind of the whole community, gathered in the presence of Christ."[32] The outworking of this principle in the Free Church tradition finds classic expression in the words of John Robinson in his sermon to the Pilgrim Church upon their departure for the New World. He reminded them that "the Lord has more truth and light yet to break forth out of his holy word."[33] As Robinson and the Plymouth congregation understood, walking together under the rule of Christ means bringing insights into the Word back to the community for conversation and testing, to discern together if it is more light or not. Reading in communion is an unfolding discernment of the mystery in Scripture. This practice of reading in community describes an interpretive process where the Spirit leads to wise readings when all are free to exercise their gifts and callings, when every voice is heard and weighed, and when no one is silenced or privileged.[34] With the Bible in our hands, we walk together in the ways made known as the Spirit leads us to ways yet to be known.[35]

Finally, some thoughts on what we can learn from Bunyan and Blake on the senses of Scripture. It is important to note that both stand within the same tradition of what literary critic Northrop Frye called "Bible-soaked" Protestantism.[36] Bunyan and Blake got the bulk of their mysterious ideas right

out of the Bible. What united them for all their differences
was a common dependence on the Bible and its framework of
construing the world that both shared.[37] Bunyan was closer to
the middle of Protestant dissent and Blake more to the radical left. Yet for neither was interpretation limited to the literal
or plain sense. They did not see the Bible as an encyclopedia
of religious information but more a set of lenses to envision
the world prophetically through a scriptural imagination. For
Bunyan, prophetic truth is better set forth in metaphors; as
he says,

> In every where so full of all these things,
> Dark Figures, Allegories, yet there springs,
> From that same Book that lustre, and those rayes
> Of light, that turns our darkest nights to days.[38]

Blake was less inclined to allegory, though he admitted it "is
seldom without some vision," and Bunyan's tale, he adds, "is
full of it."[39] Instead, Blake thought of his work as poetic imagination, and he drew his inspiration from the Bible, which he
described as "fill'd with Imagination & Visions from End to
End."[40]

In Blake's image above (figure 5), "Mercy and Truth are
Met Together, Righteousness and Peace Have Kissed Each
Other," from Psalm 85:10, which has a long tradition of allegorizing in the history of biblical interpretation pointing to
the Incarnation of Jesus Christ.[41] The inscription from Bunyan
comes from the catechesis of Christiana's sons at House Beautiful. It reminds us that there is a great deal of the Bible we
do not understand. Yet the Bible is not a problem to solve but
a mystery to discern. Bunyan himself discovered the value of
spiritual interpretation in his own experience when he thought
he might have committed the unforgiveable sin of Esau, who
despised his birthright and lost his opportunity for repentance

(Heb 12:16–17).[42] It was through spiritual (or typological) interpretation that Bunyan found comfort in seeing that the "birthright" signified "regeneration," and the "blessing" symbolized "eternal inheritance."[43] Although he had at one time despised the regenerative work of grace, in the end, he received the blessing of salvation. When he grasped that truth, Bunyan says he was freed from his fears and able to approach God with confidence.[44] Trust in God's wisdom and pray that God will lead you to discern the mystery of the Scriptures that is for your good.

Yours in search of the fuller meaning,

Interpreter

Figure 6

Great-heart: But what Ground had he for his so saying?
Honest: Why, he said he had the Scripture for his Warrant.
Great-heart: Prethee, Mr. Honest, present us with a few particulars.[1]

Mystery 5

Five Acts: The Scope of God's Story

DEAR PILGRIM:

We have already focused our attention twice on the mysteries of the nature and interpretation of Christian Scripture. I want to turn again to Scripture, this time to examine the scope of God's story. To put it simply, the Bible is the unfolding narrative of the triune God. It tells the story of God's action in creating, judging, and saving the world. The Christian canon is a collection of texts from a variety of types and styles of writing. The Bible contains many different characters and a wide range of witnesses. It has tensions, digressions, and subplots, but as a whole, it forms a coherent narrative. Scripture is God's story in which God is both the great storyteller and the primary actor. The biblical story identifies God, or more precisely, it provides an account of God's self-identification. The triune God whom Christians worship is one in the same with the God of Israel and of Jesus Christ.[2] Yet this insight only comes through the developing of divine disclosure in the unfolding story of Scripture. As Christian theologian Robert Jenson astutely observed, "God is whoever raised Jesus from the dead, having before raised Israel from Egypt."[3] To grasp the identity of God disclosed in Scripture, then, we must attend to the whole story.

The scope or the whole story, as Aristotle described it, is the movement from the beginning, to the middle, to the end.[4] While Aristotle was describing the plot of Greek tragedy, his description also fits the shape of the biblical narrative. This sense of an ending became especially important in the apocalyptic outlook of later Judaism and early Christianity. The apocalyptic plot is linear rather than circular. It moves toward an end rather than going around and around. The Christian sense of an ending drew on this vision of the world. Christian thinkers like Augustine of Hippo, writing his grand narrative *The City of God*, envisioned God as providentially guiding history toward an appointed end, unlike Homer and Plato, who imagined the world as cyclical and repetitive. The apocalyptic viewpoint provided the Christian canon with its scope—a beginning, a middle, and an end—as the biblical narrative moves toward that end. The opening line of Christian Scripture declares, "In the beginning when God created the heavens and the earth" (Gen 1:1). The final line announces, "Amen. Come, Lord Jesus!" (Rev 22:20). In the middle, the story is interrupted by the incarnation of Christ, as God "the Word became flesh and lived among us" (John 1:14).[5]

Focusing on the sense of an ending can have radical and even dangerous consequences if the biblical narrative is taken as a manifesto for anarchism and revolution.[6] The end, however, can be a generative source for living. The literary critic and author J. R. R. Tolkien famously described the arc of the Christian story as bent toward what he called *euchatastrophe*, a happy ending, rather than *apocalypse*, the final destruction of all things. To believe that in Christ, God has moved the world toward this happy ending is not escapism, nor does it deny the existence of sorrow or failure. It does deny, however, that unhappiness is the final word. It hopes that the end of the story is not defeat but a sudden and miraculous grace that intervenes for good. The consolation of a joyous ending, Tolkien argued, is not just the stuff of myth and fairy tales. The decisive turn of events at the end is good news, and it is fundamental to the gospel. Approaching the Christian story from this viewpoint results in the joyous sense that God has redeemed the world's corruption in a strange yet happy way. From this standpoint, the incarnation of Christ is the *euchatastrophe* of human history, and the resurrection of Christ is the *euchatastrophe* of the incarnation. The Christian story begins and ends in joy as it looks forward and backward to that great *euchatastrophe*.[7]

While the focus of the biblical narrative is eschatological, its account of life is also realistic. The Bible does not present the story of an otherworldly reality, unknown and unknowable to human experience. There is a history-like (or mimetic) quality to its narrative. As we have already examined, one of the great testimonies to the truth of the Bible is that it has elicited a vast tradition of spiritual interpretation while never doing away with the literal (or plain) sense. This realistic representation of biblical narrative, however, has often led modern readers to mistake the literal with the factual so that the plain sense disappears. For example, the Synoptic Gospels all recount the story about Jesus casting demons out of a man and sending them into a herd of pigs, which rushed over a cliff into the Sea of Galilee and drowned. The Gospels, however, have different names for the scene. Mark and Luke place it near the town of Gerasa, which is about thirty-seven miles from the Sea of Galilee (Mark 5:1; Luke 8:26), and Matthew locates it near Gadara, which is only five miles away (Matt 8:28). Some manuscripts, reflecting concern about the conflicting locations, even change the name to Gergasa, which makes geographic sense because it is very near the shore of the Sea. Gerasa, however, is the strongest attested reading, but that would seem to leave us with the problem of explaining how the demonic pigs ran almost forty miles to jump into the sea. One commentator explains the disagreement by proposing that the word *Gerasa* derives from the Hebrew word that means "to banish" and is associated with exorcism.[8] It makes sense that Mark might want to make a theological point by connecting the region linguistically related to exorcism and the exorcism story.

The truth of the story, however, does not hinge on geography. Indeed, the problem arises when we mistake the history-likeness of the biblical narrative for direct reference to historical events. More importantly, such an error in reading misses the underlying agreement in all three accounts, namely, that the Synoptic Gospels provide identical identifications of Jesus as the Son of God, who exercises power over the demonic spirits. The Evangelists are more concerned that we understand the identity of God's Messiah than we know the topography of Palestine because the question we must confront is whether the Christ we meet in the Gospels still exercises the power to transform troubled souls into people of sound mind.[9]

We must learn to be careful readers who do not simply conflate the literal sense of the biblical narrative with the factual reality of the natural world because there is more going on in the Bible than just history and geography. Confusing the literal with the factual tempts us to reduce the message to principles so that there is no further need to refer to the text, resulting in "the eclipse of biblical narrative."[10] Yet as the eminent literary critic Erich Auerbach perceptively noted, the Bible does not simply claim to be *historically true*. It insists that the world it portrays is *exclusively true*, not simply a narrated reality that distracts us for a short time from our existence but the only real world. In reading the Scriptures, we confront, or, rather, we are confronted by the mysterious God, who asserts absolute authority and demands total submission.[11] We may recoil from such an audacious claim, but there is no escaping the fact that the identity of God is inseparable from the entire scope of biblical narrative. To put it simply, the whole Bible is an identity narrative because we learn from the story who God is.

Christian Scripture identifies God. Sometimes the identification is indirect, like the prophet Isaiah's characterization of God enthroned in the temple with angels crying, "Holy, holy, holy is the Lord of hosts" (Isa 6:3). Although Isaiah never actually tells us "God is holy," his response of overwhelming awe in the presence of such a profound mystery leaves little question that this is the case.[12] In other passages, God's identification is more direct. For example, God declares to Israel, "I the Lord your God am holy" (Lev 19:2). We do not have to wonder who God is because God self-identifies as "the holy One of Israel." Yet it is not at all clear what this declaration means simply from that one sentence. To understand what God's holiness means requires a sustained engagement with the biblical story. By continuing to read, we discover that God's holiness signifies a danger zone. We learn that being close to God is not a safe place. When Moses goes up Mt. Sinai to meet with God, Moses sets a boundary, warning that anyone who even touches the mountain "shall be put to death" (Exod 19:12). As we carry on reading, we learn that the holiness of God has implications for the people of God. The holiness of God requires a holy people: "You shall be holy, for I the Lord your God am holy" (Lev 19:2). Israel's holiness must be enacted in the way the people live. That enacted holiness includes detailed dietary instructions. Yet the restriction of what Israelites may and may not eat is not based on hygienic or health reasons but entirely as a sign that they are God's people. Every aspect of life must conform to God. The weight of this awesome responsibility would be too much for ordinary human beings to bear, except that being set apart to serve this holy God is a gift. It is the way of life, and God, this holy One, is the source of life.[13]

As Israel falteringly followed in the way of life, God sent prophets like Jeremiah, Ezekiel, and Micah to guide them as wandering sheep back into the fold (Jer 50:6; Ezek 34:23–24; Micah 5:4–5). The prophets were followed by Jesus, Israel's Messiah, whose mission was to lead the lost sheep of Israel back into the way (Matt 10:6). Though the earliest followers of Jesus were Jewish, remarkably, people outside Israel became followers of the way. These Gentile believers were also committed to a life of holiness; as the Scripture states, "You shall be holy, for I am holy" (1 Pet 1:16). Those who follow the Good Shepherd are "a peculiar people" (1 Pet 2:9, KJV). Yet the question arose in the early days of Christianity whether Gentile followers of the way must keep holiness in the same way as Israel. After much deliberation, the early church leaders discerned that Gentile believers should not be required to observe the code of holiness as prescribed in the Old Testament. Addressing the assembly of the elders in Jerusalem, the apostle Peter implored:

> My brothers, you know that in the early days God made a choice among you, that I should be the one through whom the Gentiles would hear the message of the good news and become believers. And God, who knows the human heart, testified to them by giving them the Holy Spirit, just as he did to us; and in cleansing their hearts by faith he has made no distinction between them and us. Now therefore why are you putting God to the test by placing on the neck of the disciples a yoke that neither our ancestors nor we have been able to bear? On the contrary, we believe that we will be saved through the grace of the Lord Jesus, just as they will. (Acts 15:7–11)

James the apostle replied that the inclusion of the Gentiles was not a new idea but instead was God's plan for the rebuilding of Israel (Acts 15:13–18). The full participation of Gentiles did not mean the Holy One of Israel and the God of Jesus Christ were two different characters. These two are one and the same God, but the only way to arrive at that awareness is to follow the story from beginning to end. God's identity unfolds in a developing narrative. For that reason, it is important to read the whole story and to attend in particular to God's self-disclosure.

One way to grasp the scope of God's story is to read the Bible as a five-act drama.[14] The biblical canon dramatically organized might look something like this.

Act 1 Creation—Genesis 1–11
Act 2 Covenant—Genesis 12–Deuteronomy, Prophets,
                    Writings
Act 3 Christ—Four Gospels
Act 4 Church—Acts, Paul's Letters, and
                    General Epistles
Act 5 Consummation—Revelation

Together, these five acts name the arc or scope of the biblical narrative. Conceived as theodrama, the Bible is the comprehensive story of God's action from creation to consummation.[15] The Christian Scriptures are an expression of God's self-disclosure and a description of the divine economy. The fullness of God's identity is not revealed all at once because the divine performance accommodates the limitations of a human audience. God is the Trinity, but the first act does not begin with the full disclosure of God as three in one. Yet it is nevertheless true to describe the Bible as the unfolding story of the triune God. That characterization, however, comes gradually. Only over the course of the performance does it become clear that the God who made the world by the Word *is* the Word (Gen 1:3) made flesh in Christ (John 1:14), the first and the last, the Alpha and the Omega (Rev 22:13), and that the Spirit of God who moved on the face of the waters at creation (Gen 1:2) is the same Spirit who invites us in the end to drink freely of the water of life (Rev 22:17). Each act discloses more of the divine identity, and each act presupposes the previous ones as the plot unfolds.

Act 1 begins in silence and darkness. Then there is a sound. God speaks, "Let there be light" (Gen 1:3). These words do not just state. They create. They do not simply say something. They do something.[16] God's Word does not merely describe or report. God's Word makes something happen. God's Word generates. God's speech is like an umpire who says, "Play ball!" or a judge who says, "Case dismissed!" God's Word is not just a *constantive* or *descriptive* statement. It is a *performative* utterance. God's Word does not simply declare an old truth. It initiates a new reality. God's Word makes a world. It is no accident that the Psalmist declares, "By the word of the Lord the heavens were made" (Ps 33:6). Nor is it surprising that the fourth Gospel opens,

> In the beginning was the Word, and the Word was with God, and the Word was God. He was in the beginning with God. All things came into being through him, and without him not one thing came into being. (John 1:1–3)

The emphasis of Act 1, however, is not on the creation by itself but on the Creator, who by the Word brings the world into being. God's Word creates, but more importantly, the Word God discloses who the Creator is, yet why God would make the world in the first place remains a mystery. God did not need to create. God created simply because God loves infinitely and freely, but even the love that moves the sun and the stars could not prevent humanity's refusal of love or the travail of creation that followed.[17]

Act 2 opens in the wake of God's failure to hold the sons and daughters of earth in close relationship. Yet God, who loves freely, is unhindered. God begins by making a covenant promise to Noah and his descendants (Gen 9:8) by putting a rainbow in the cloud as a sign (Gen 9:12) so that the sign would be a remembrance of the covenant (Gen 9:15–16). The action continues with God making a covenant promise with Abraham and his children (Gen 15:18, 17:7). When distress comes to them, God remembers the covenant with Abraham, Isaac, and Jacob (Exod 2:24). And when the people of Israel, the children of Jacob and Leah, are enslaved in Egypt, God promises them, "I hereby make a covenant" (Exod 34:10) and adds, "I will remember in their favor the covenant with their ancestors whom I brought out of the land of Egypt in the sight of the nations, to be their God" (Lev 26:45). Act 2 tells the story of God's steadfast and unfailing love:

> He is mindful of his covenant forever,
> > of the word that he commanded, for a thousand
> > generations,
> the covenant that he made with Abraham,
> > his sworn promise to Isaac,
> which he confirmed to Jacob as a statute,
> > to Israel as an everlasting covenant. (Ps 105:8–10)

Act 2 is the story of Israel, who, like its ancestor Jacob, wrestles with God (Gen 32:28), but more importantly, it tells the story of such relentless pursuit that we wonder who this One is whose love will not let Israel go. God's love and God's identity, however, remain a mystery, even to Moses. "I am who I am" (Exod 3:14), God announces from the burning bush, which means something like "I will always be ahead of you. Find me as you follow the journey."[18] God's faithfulness to be in covenant relationship with Israel does not end with the people of Israel but with a desire that they may be a light to all the nations (Isa 60:3) and bring all creation into harmony with their source of life. Yet as Act 2 closes, Israel wanders, despite God's free and faithful love, leading us to wonder if God might find another way.

Act 3 is the central action in the drama. Christ stands in the middle of the story, between Israel and the church (Luke 4:16ff, 16:16, Acts 10:38).[19] God called Israel to be a covenant partner in a journey on the way that is life (Deut 30:19). When Israel faltered and went into exile, God remembered the promise. The prophets envisioned God making a way (Isa 40:3–5) and preparing to do a new thing (Isa 43:19). The last prophet in the Old Testament canon, Malachi, declared that the Lord's messenger would clear the way for God personally to enter the temple (Mal 3:1). Mark's Gospel opens with those prophetic words, identifying John the Baptist as God's messenger preparing the way (Mark 1:3). The Gospel of John makes an even more startling claim: The Word by which God created the world was made flesh in Jesus (John 1:1–14). He does not simply call followers into the way. He is the way (John 14:6). Yet the way leads to the cross, where, when his hour had finally come and his work was complete, he offered himself as a sacrifice, breathing out his life-giving Spirit, bringing new life out of suffering and death (John 19:30–34). There on the cross, love incarnate becomes vulnerable to the powers of death, but death cannot finally block the way. Nonetheless, Act 3 does not end with the death of God's Messiah. In the final scene, Jesus is "declared to be Son of God with power according to the spirit of holiness by resurrection from the dead" (Rom 1:4). Still the drama does not end with Act 3.

Act 4 continues the story. The risen Christ ascends into heaven (Acts 1:9), and the Holy Spirit descends on the church

(Acts 2:4). By the Spirit, the Lord continues to be present with his people. Though Christ is no longer physically present, the Spirit equips and empowers the church to be the body of Christ in the world. Upon confession of their faith and commitment to follow the way, they enter the waters of baptism and are incorporated into the body and become participants in the drama (Acts 8:38). Those who follow Jesus, the way incarnate, become known as people of the way (Acts 9:2). God declares the church, the assembly of the faithful, to be "a chosen people, a royal priesthood, a holy nation, God's own people" (1 Pet 2:9). They devote themselves "to the apostles' teaching and fellowship, to the breaking of bread and the prayers" (Acts 2:42). When they perform the Eucharist by remembering Jesus and invoking the Spirit, Christ makes himself really and personally known in the breaking of bread (1 Cor 11:23–26). The remembrance of Jesus stands in continuity with the historic covenant language that pleads for God to act decisively to complete the work of salvation already begun in Jesus. The Lord's Supper is a performative act of common prayer by the church. It recalls as a memorial before the Father the unique sacrifice of the Son and invokes God's abiding presence through the Spirit. In doing so, it prefigures and indeed hastens the very future it signifies. Through the Spirit, the church becomes a witness to Christ unto the ends of the earth (Acts 1:8) and until the end of the age (Matt 28:19–20). But the drama is not over.

Act 5 is the end of the story and the final act of the drama. Each celebration of the Lord's Supper proclaims "the Lord's death until he comes" (1 Cor 11:26). Gathered at the table, God's people lift up a prayer shared through the ages with the earliest Christians: *Marana'tha*—"Come Lord!" (1 Cor 16:22).[20] Yet we do not know the timing of the end. As Jesus warned, "But about that day or hour no one knows, neither the angels in heaven nor the Son, but only the Father" (Mark 13:32). God in God's time will bring the end. There will be resurrection and judgment, a new heaven and a new earth, even a new Jerusalem. As the One seated on the throne announces, "See, I am making all things new" (Rev 21:5). When the end comes, God, who has been concealed, even when revealed, will be fully known. And here is the good news: The God whose identity will be unveiled at the end will be the same God who was veiled in the beginning, and the God who will be disclosed in the final act will be identical with the God we have met in Jesus Christ. For "the face on the cross is the face on the throne."[21] So we wait with patience and hope, living out the story, participating in the drama, performing the script, repeating the practices of the faith with the faithful "until he comes." Let the church say, "Amen. Come, Lord Jesus! The grace of the Lord Jesus be with all the saints. Amen" (Rev 22:20–21).

There is always a temptation to pull out of the drama, presuming to know the mind of the Almighty. The final curtain, however, has yet to fall. We are still in the middle, discerning the mystery. The greatness of the biblical narrative, as Nicholas Lash observed, "lies in its inexhaustible capacity . . . to dramatize fundamental features of the human drama."[22] We must continue to engage in the performance of the divine script. For only by practicing the lines, enacting the parts, and participating in the drama will we grow in our insight into the scope of God's story.

The epigraph from Bunyan recalls a conversation between Old Honest and Mr. Great-heart, who recount the confusion of Mr. Selfwill, a professed pilgrim whose petulant lack of understanding of the scope of Scripture led to his undoing. Blake's illustration at the head of this chapter (figure 6) further warns against the mistake of hermeneutical impatience.[23] Trusting

in the conviction that he is a person of integrity, Job continues his protest. He suffers, yet he claims innocence. He does
not give up on God, though he is certain that somehow God
must be responsible for his struggle. At last, God appears in a
whirlwind and answers Job: "Who is this that darkens counsel by words without knowledge?" (Job 38:2). God exposes
Job's ignorance of the scope of creation and providence. God's
speech and vision transform Job, who confesses:

> I have uttered what I did not understand,
> things too wonderful for me that I did not know.
> (Job 42:3)

Karl Barth described Job as a "true witness" to God's freedom
by respecting God's freedom to give and to take away, yet to
do so with a defiant resignation that insists that God ought to
have exercised infinite freedom quite differently.[24] Job exemplifies the faithful struggle of God's companions, who in the
midst of the divine drama seek to bear truthful witness to
the mystery of God's will and way. Let us then learn to wait
patiently like Job until the coming of the Lord (Jas 5:7–11).

Yours in enduring hope,
Interpreter

Figure 7

Through all my Life thy favour is
So frankly shew'd to me,
That in thy House for evermore
My dwelling place shall be.[1]

Mystery 6

Six Seasons: The Church Year

Dear Pilgrim:

Calendars and clocks are amazing tools. They enable us to keep time by measuring and marking the temporal continuum through which we move. With their help, we can plot our chronological course by dividing time into segments—years, months, days, hours, seconds, even nanoseconds. One of the innovations that revolutionized time-keeping is the worldwide system of time zones. The universal standardization of time had far-reaching consequences, making regional, national, and international connections more efficient. By creating a global standard of time, accurate and efficient synchronization around the world became possible. Imagine life without a sense of time. Yet as Christians we learn to mark time by another method. Robinson Crusoe realized after he landed on a deserted island that if he lost track of time, he might not be able to distinguish Sabbath days from working days. He quickly set out to make a calendar out of a large wooden post, which he erected on the beach where he landed. His reckoning of time began with the date of his arrival. Each day, he cut a notch with his knife, grouping the marks to indicate weeks, months, and years.[2] Crusoe's calendar gave him a sense of rhythm and purpose. It also connected him with civilization, from which the waters of the sea separated him. Keeping time made him aware that though he was isolated on an island, he was not alone in the world.

Temporal experience has many social implications, but an often overlooked aspect of time is its spiritual dimension, which clocks and calendars cannot measure or explain. The meaning of time may seem obvious at first, but the longer we think about it, the more we become aware that we are approaching something mysterious. "What is time?" Saint Augustine muses in his *Confessions*. "If no one asks me, I know; if I want to explain it to someone who does ask me, I do not know."[3] Augustine is right. Time defies explanation. It is complex, not simple. There is not just one time. There are three times: the present memory of the past, the present intuition of the present, and the present expectation of the future.[4] Augustine's extended meditation led him to confront his inability to understand the nature of time. We face the same mystery. Although we are aware of time, our consciousness cannot grasp the fullness of time because it is constantly changing, passing away from anticipation, to sight, to memory. Time, Augustine argues, is not a problem to solve but a mystery to discern. For all time coexists in God, who is eternally present.[5] Human beings are temporal, but God is eternal. Augustine's confession thus ends where it began: we must pass through intervals on our temporal journey until we finally rest in the mystery of the eternal and unchanging God, who is present in all time.[6]

While the *chronological rendering of time* has attracted the interest of modern minds, it is the *theological reckoning of time* that has been the particular focus for Jews and Christians. As Rabbi Abraham Joshua Heschel observed, "Judaism is a religion of time aiming at the sanctification of time."[7] The biblical accounting of time does not begin with the cycles of nature. It begins with God. The book of Genesis says, "God blessed the seventh day and hallowed it, because on it God rested from all the work that he had done in creation" (Gen 2:3). Moreover, because God sanctified the Sabbath, God commanded Israel, "Remember the Sabbath day and keep it holy" (Exod 20:8). Time is God's gift to the world, and God challenged Israel to mark the holiness of time by keeping the Sabbath as a day of rest. The Sabbath, however, is not merely a day to refrain from work. It is a time of restful celebration for body and soul. The book of Acts indicates that the earliest followers of Christ, who were Jewish, initially continued to worship and pray in the way of Israel (Acts 3:1). As the Christian witness extended from Jerusalem, to Judea and Samaria, to the ends of the earth (Acts 1:8), the day of worship gradually shifted from Saturday to Sunday. Ignatius of Antioch and other early Christian observers suggest that by the second century, the "mystery" of Christ so transformed the lives of Jewish and Gentile believers that they stopped observing the Sabbath and began to worship on the Lord's Day.[8]

Some followers of Christ still worship on Saturday, although most Christians gather on Sunday, "the first day of the week" (1 Cor 16:2), because Sunday was the day of the Lord's resurrection (Mark 16:2) and because the risen Lord met with his disciples on the day of the resurrection and on the following Sunday (John 20:1, 19). Christians affirm the holiness of time, not only by remembering that God is Creator of all things but by celebrating "the Lord's day" (Rev 1:10) that signifies the new creation that has come in Christ (2 Cor 5:17). Yet even though we may worship on Sunday, we recognize that this day is not like the others. Sunday is a Sabbath. As Christian theologian Jürgen Moltmann explains, "The Christian Sunday neither abolishes Israel's Sabbath nor supplants it." Instead, he continues, the Lord's Day "must be seen as the

messianic extension of Israel's Sabbath."[9] The Sabbath regula-
tions that guided Israel find fulfillment in the person of Jesus.
My colleague Norman Wirzba says it well: "If we want to see,
hear, feel, taste, and touch what God's delight in creation con-
cretely amounts to, we can do no better than to consider the
life and ministry of Jesus Christ."[10] The keeping of Sunday
as the Lord's Day marks our commitment to sanctify time
because we believe God has sanctified time in the new creation. By setting aside one day to commemorate the creative
and transformative mystery of God, we seek to discern "Easter
in ordinary."[11]

The early Christians modeled the season of Holy Week and
Easter after the Jewish Passover, the holiest of days in Israel. The
apostle Paul describes Christ as "our paschal lamb," who "has
been sacrificed" (1 Cor 5:7), and the Synoptic Gospels present the Last Supper as a Passover meal with Christ's suffering
and death also portrayed as a Christian Pascha. John's Gospel
makes an even more striking connection by noting that Jesus
was tried before Pilate on the Day of Preparation for Passover
and was handed over to be crucified at noon, the very moment
when the priests would have begun the slaughter of the paschal lambs in the temple (John 19:13–16). The second-century
Christian bishop Melitio of Sardis suggested that the worship
of the church is the enactment of the paschal mystery:

> The mystery of the Pascha is . . . old with respect to
> the law, new with respect to the word. Provisional with
> respect to the type, yet everlasting through grace. It is
> perishable because of the slaughter of the sheep, imper-
> ishable because of the life of the Lord. It is mortal
> because of the burial in the ground, immortal because of
> the resurrection from the dead.[12]

Although Melitio notes that the word *Pascha* literally means
"suffering," he makes it clear that this suffering is not limited to

Christ's death on the cross but rather includes the entire course of his earthly life from birth to ascension.[13] As the Heidelberg Catechism puts it, Christ suffered "his whole life on earth, but especially at the end" as the atoning sacrifice to deliver us from sin and gain for us eternal life.[14] The paschal mystery in this fuller sense is the heart of Christian worship. Although the passion of Christ is a historical event, wherever two or three are gathered in his name, the paschal mystery becomes a present reality through word and sacrament, just as Christ promised (Matt 18:20).[15]

Reaching agreement on the observance of an annual Easter celebration, however, was a struggle that took several centuries to resolve. Church leaders in Asia Minor like Polycarp, the second-century bishop of Smyrna, were influenced by the practice of the apostle John, who observed Pascha as a memorial of the death of Jesus on the fourteenth day of Nisan (Exod 12:1–6), the first month of the year according to the Jewish calendar. Because that timetable followed the lunar cycle, the Pascha memorial might occur any day of the week. Christians in Rome and the West, influenced by the apostles Peter and Paul, followed a different practice. They observed Easter, always on Sunday, and not as a memorial to Christ's death but as a celebration of his resurrection. Gradually, the observance of Pascha/Easter shifted from a memorial of the death of Christ to the celebration of the resurrection. In 325 AD, the Council of Nicaea determined that the celebration of Pascha/Easter should occur on the first Sunday after the first full moon after the spring equinox. Yet differences in the calculation of the observance have persisted. Although all Christians follow the Nicene formulation, because Catholics and Protestants base their calculations of Easter on the more accurate Gregorian calendar, and the Orthodox Church depends on the less accurate and older Julian calendar, the celebrations of Easter and Pascha rarely coincide.[16]

The celebration of a little Easter every Sunday and a Great Sunday on Easter are ancient practices that have helped Christians learn how to keep time as Christians. The Easter-Sunday pattern assists in learning to reckon life by God's time, not just the clock or the calendar. Christians gradually developed a fuller way of shaping the entire year around the pattern of God's time. Observing the Christian year attends more intentionally to the unfolding narrative in Scripture as the church enacts God's story in the six seasons of Advent, Christmas, Epiphany, Lent, Easter, and Pentecost. The church year is not about measuring time but about discerning it. Scripture and the Christian year both tell God's story, but each differently. The structure of biblical narrative is *epic*. The form of the church year is *lyric*. The biblical story is linear. It moves from beginning, to middle, to end. The Christian year is cyclical, although not a circle that loops back to the beginning and starts all over again. It is more of a spiral, like the thread of a screw that draws our lives deeper into the life of God. The cycle of the Christian year has a trinitarian pattern. From Advent through Christmas, the focus is on the Father's gift. From Lent through Easter, the attention is on the Son's sacrifice. From Pentecost through Ordinary time, the emphasis is on the Spirit's indwelling presence.

When I was a young pastor just beginning my ministry, I attended a conference led by a popular Methodist preacher and theologian.[17] He knew many of the attendees like me were from evangelical rather than liturgical churches that did not observe the Christian year. Our services typically ended with an altar call where the preacher invited people to come forward and confess their faith in Christ. He commended our evangelical commitment to preaching the cross every Sunday, but he added, "The Christian year is more than fifty-two Good Fridays." He provocatively suggested that the worship calendar of many churches was more attentive to national holidays,

denominational offerings, and Hallmark cards than to the
Christian faith. He intoned, "No wonder so many churches
are more committed to the preservation of the United States
of America than to the mission of Jesus Christ." Then he laid
out a challenge: "If you want your congregations to be the
church of Jesus Christ, you could start by following the Christian year." He argued that the rhythm of the Christian year
teaches us what it means not to be conformed to the world
but to be transformed by the renewing of our minds that we
may discern the good, acceptable, and perfect will of God
(Rom 12:2). As much as I hated to admit it, deep in my heart I
knew he was right. My life and my ministry were determined
not by Christian time but by national time. Thanksgiving is
not Christian time. Mother's Day is not Christian time. July
Fourth is not Christian time. Not even Christmas and Easter
as cultural and commercial observances are Christian time. I
began to explore the necessary changes to convert my life and
my ministry to Christian time. It was not easy.

The Free Church tradition that shaped my faith empha-
sizes that worship is listening to what the risen Lord through
the Spirit is saying (Rev 2:7). We believe worship is free
because "the Lord is the Spirit, and where the Spirit of the
Lord is, there is freedom" (2 Cor 3:17). This emphasis on spiritual worship as freedom has sometimes produced resistance
to the use of set prayers, assigned texts, and fixed patterns.
John Smyth, the first Baptist, contended that worship must
be extemporaneous to be truly spiritual. He argued that reciting memorized words or reading written prayers quenches the
Spirit. He stated that one comes from the mind, the other
from a book, but neither arises from the heart, and "in neither
of them the Spirit is at liberty."[18] John Bunyan contended that
a true worship is "sincere, sensible, affectionate pouring out of
the heart or soul to God, through Christ, in the strength and
assistance of the Holy Spirit."[19] The conviction of the liberty

of spiritual worship is so strong that some even refuse to recite the Lord's Prayer (Matt 6:9–13), referencing Jesus's critique of hypocritical religiosity and the use of "empty phrases" (Matt 6:5–7). Others appeal to the apostle Paul's rebuke of the Galatian Christians for "observing special days and months and seasons and years" (Gal 4:10). I do not share the belief that to be spiritual, worship must be iconoclastic. I have found that as I freely embraced the forms of liturgical worship, and in particular the more closely I began to follow the Christian year, the more liberated I became and the more spiritual the worship I experienced.

The liturgical calendar and the texts in the revised common lectionary are tools that provide order for the spiritual life that teaches us to live by God's time. The sights, sounds, smells, tastes, and feelings of the seasons open our senses to the reality of God's life-giving presence, whom we worship with our whole being "in spirit and truth" (John 4:24). Marking time by participating in the rich traditions of the seasons reaching back to ancient Christianity opens us to discern the unfolding of the mystery of Christ. For as John Calvin rightly observed, "Christ has redeemed us . . . by the whole course of his obedience."[20] In Advent, we prepare for the promise of Christ's coming. In Christmas, we celebrate the wonder of Christ's birth. In Epiphany, we behold Christ's manifestation to the whole world. In Lent, we follow Christ's journey toward death. In Easter, we rejoice in Christ's resurrection from the dead. In Pentecost, we look to Christ's living presence through the Spirit.[21] Following the liturgical year forms Christian identity through the sacred ordering of time that resists the power of secular interests. It frames the Christian vision to look for what God is doing in the world rather than seeking ways to maintain control. It fosters ecumenical cooperation by sharing the journey with fellow Christians in the wider church around the world and over time. It frees us to participate more fully in the divine drama as we enact God's story in worship, work, and witness. Most importantly, it focuses our attention on the unfolding mystery of Christ, the Alpha and Omega, in whom the eternal Word became flesh in time.

The annunciation to the shepherds (Luke 2:8–20) appears in the lectionary readings for Christmas in Year C. One of the challenges of rehearsing the Christmas story is to hear the good news that, as the Nicene Creed affirms, "for us and for our salvation [Christ] came down from heaven, was incarnate of the Holy Spirit and the Virgin Mary and became truly human."[22] We do not have to wait for the cross and resurrection for our salvation. We are saved because "the Word became flesh and lived among us" (John 1:14). Athanasius of Alexandria likened the mystery of redemption to a king who enters a city and dwells in one of its houses, thereby saving the whole city by his presence. So it is when the King of the universe entered our world and dwelt in one body that the whole human race was saved by his life.[23]

William Blake's picture of the annunciation of the nativity (figure 7) helps us to imagine how we might receive this as good news today. His rendering of the scene shows the shepherds kneeling in wonder as the angels announce the Savior's birth. Their faces are uplifted as rays of light bathe the gathering, illuminating their vision of the nativity in the distance. In the heavenly light, they see the new creation in the fullness of Christ's life that reverses the law of sin and death. Blake's illustration appeared in John Milton's poem on the nativity, which reads:

At last surrounds their sight
A globe of circular light,
  That with long beams the shamefaced Night arrayed;
The helmèd Cherubim
And sworded Seraphim,
  Are seen in glittering ranks with wings displayed,

Harping in loud and solemn quire,
With unexpressive notes to Heaven's newborn Heir.[24]

Because Christ made his dwelling among us, we will live forever with the Lord. With Christian pilgrims ancient and future, let us then lift our voices in praise to God:

Through all my Life thy favour is
So frankly shew'd to me,
That in thy House for evermore
My dwelling place shall be.[25]

Yours in living by God's time,
Interpreter

Figure 8

Then they had her to a place, and shewed her Jacob's Ladder. Now at that time there were some Angels ascending upon it. So Christiania looked and looked, to see the Angels go up, and so did the rest of the Company.[1]

Mystery 7

Seven Sacramental Signs: Holy Things for Holy People

DEAR PILGRIM:

"Sacraments are what you do in church. What you do at home is something else."[2] That is how ten-year-old Virginia Cary Hudson began her essay on the sacraments. It makes sense that preparing a meal and taking a bath are not sacraments, but being baptized and receiving communion are. Sacraments are holy things, but their elements are ordinary. We recognize words, water, bread, and wine. They are common things in our everyday experience. We know how they look, sound, smell, taste, and feel. Yet there is something different about these things when we use them in church. They are not just words and water or bread and wine. They become powerful signs that signify a reality beyond their material form. These ordinary things are transformed into holy things that God uses for a sacred purpose.[3] The distinction between ordinary things and holy things has a long tradition. In the ancient Christian liturgy, the bishop invited people to participate in the Eucharist with the words "Holy things for holy people."[4] Not everyone was welcomed at the sacred meal. Admittance to communion, to become a partaker of the divine mysteries, was a privilege reserved for the baptized.[5] They had been instructed in the way of holiness (1 Pet 1:13–14). They were born anew by the living Word of God (1 Pet 1:22–23). They might not have been perfect, but they were going on toward perfection (Heb 6:1).

The Protestant Reformation blurred the lines between holy and ordinary. Martin Luther declared that "we are all priests, as many of us as are Christians."[6] The notion of ordinary priesthood called for a rethinking and reordering of church and society. The priesthood of all believers elevated ordinary life, opening up the possibility of everyday work as a holy vocation. It also empowered the laity to subvert the prescriptive power and stratified ordering by ecclesial and civil authorities, which otherwise would have determined their lives and relations. Everyday practices thus became means of reforming church and society. Luther famously praised fathers who defied socially prescribed gender roles to perform seemingly menial domestic tasks like washing dirty diapers, describing them as examples of a Christian ministry and adding, "God, with all his angels and creatures, is smiling, not because that father is washing diapers, but because he is doing so in Christian faith."[7] When transformed by the gospel, everyday practices like parenting, cooking, and washing become modes of Christian witness. They disrupt the schematic ordering of the world produced through the strategic practices of the powerful, and they provide ordinary means to contest the social order.[8]

Ordinary practices such as preparing food, cooking meals, serving guests, and doing the dishes can also be ways for us to see God at work. The repetitiveness of ordinary things can become occasions for us to see how God might be active in the uncommon and extraordinary gift of holy things if we are open to the possibility of commonplace tasks as instruments of divine action. The poet and author Kathleen Norris describes how her experience in everyday practices became a window into the mysteries of the gospel. Seeing the priest "as a kind of daft housewife, overdressed for the kitchen, in bulky robes, puttering about the altar, washing up after having served so great a meal to so many people" opened her eyes to the mystery of Holy Communion.[9] The everyday practice of eating opens our eyes to discern the holy mystery. We pray, "Give us today our daily bread" (Matt 6:11), knowing that "One does not live by bread alone, but by every word that comes from the mouth of God" (Matt 4:4). Yet we witness ordinary bread as holy when it becomes God's Word of life for us. Holy things are not puzzles to decipher. They are mysteries to receive. Yet holy things are made holy from ordinary things. The Word became flesh. Christ was born in a manger. Jesus is present in bread and wine. God speaks through human words. The Holy Spirit renews us in the water of rebirth.

There is a deep connection as well as a vast distinction between the ordinary and the holy. One way we recognize that difference is the name the church gives these holy things. They are sacraments. Christians differ about how many there are. The Catholic Church observes the seven sacraments of baptism, confirmation, Eucharist, penance, the anointing of the sick, holy orders, and marriage, while Protestants typically practice only baptism and the Lord's Supper as sacraments. Naming and numbering the sacraments is important, but perhaps even weightier is the matter of what sacraments actually do. One purpose of sacraments is to signify. The catechism of the Episcopal Church describes sacraments as "outward and visible signs of inward and spiritual grace."[10] Thinking about sacraments as outward signs of invisible sacred things goes back to Saint Augustine.[11] "These realities," he explained, "are called sacraments because in them one thing is seen, while another is grasped. What is seen is a mere physical likeness; what is grasped bears spiritual fruit."[12] Signs signify things, and context determines the ways we see signs. Suppose we decide to play a game of baseball, and you take off your hat, drop it on the ground, and say, "This is first base." It would make no sense for me to say, "That is not literally first base. It is literally a hat but really first base." In the context of that game, it *is* first base, really and literally. However, when you get home, if your mother asks you to take off your hat, it would make no sense to say, "This is not a hat. It is first base." How we use a sign determines its meaning. When we are eating a meal at home, bread and wine are bread and wine, but when we are observing the Lord's Supper in church, bread and wine are not just bread and wine. They are the body and blood of Christ.

Sacraments are signs that point to something beyond themselves. They are ordinary things that signify holy things. The *Westminster Catechism* calls them not just signs but "sensible signs."[13] As humans, we communicate with other humans through words uttered from our mouths. We also communicate through gestures like handshakes, hugs, and smiles. Sacraments are God's ways of communicating. They are signs by which God communes with us.[14] My theological mentor Jim McClendon distinguished three types of signs through which God speaks: historic signs, providential signs, and remembering signs.[15] God communicates through great signs in the history of redemption, from the burning bush to the empty tomb to the flaming tongues of fire. God also speaks to us through providential signs like answered prayers, heightened affections, or a still small voice. God guides and encourages us in the faith journey through historic and providential signs, but neither is repeatable. Remembering signs, however, are repetitive actions through which God continues to speak. The remembering signs of preaching, baptism, and table connect the story of the once-for-all historic signs to believers and believing communities around the world and over time. By repeating these remembering signs, we draw on the language that Israel and the church have used to recall God's past redemption as historically exemplified, to trust God's present deliverance as sacramentally signified, and to envision God's coming salvation as eschatologically anticipated.

Sacraments are signs, but they are not empty or arbitrary signs. They are effective signs or means of grace. As the great medieval theologian Peter Lombard observed, "A sacrament is properly so called because it is a sign of God's grace and a form of invisible grace in such manner that it bears its image and is its cause." He adds, "The sacraments were not instituted only for the sake of signifying, but also to sanctify."[16] The relation between the sign and the thing signified is neither mechanical nor magical. Our words and actions do not cause God to be present. As John Calvin put it, "A sacrament is never without a preceding promise but is joined to it as a sort of appendix, with the purpose of confirming and sealing the promise itself, and of making it more evident to us and in a sense ratifying it."[17] Something is sacramental because God promises to be present in and through the performance of the words, actions, and reception. It is a sacrament because it is "a sign through and in which God freely accomplishes that which is signified, not in a manner that can be presumed or manipulated, but in a manner that is truly gracious."[18] In his baptistic adaptation of the Heidelberg Catechism, Hercules Collins defined the sacraments as "sacred signs and seals, set before our eyes, and ordained of God for this cause, that he may declare and seal by them the promise of his gospel to us."[19] William Kiffin, a seventeenth-century English Baptist pastor and church leader, stated that the Lord's Supper "is a spiritual participation of the body and blood of Christ by faith" and so "is a means of salvation."[20] He sounded a warning against anti-sacramental theology, saying that anyone who does not care for "Christ sacramental; cares as little for Christ God, Christ flesh, Christ

Emanuel," adding "by these he comes near."[21] An old Baptist confession of faith affirms the power of the sacraments succinctly, saying as Israel "had the manna to nourish them in the wilderness to Canaan; so have we the sacraments, to nourish us in the church, and in our wilderness-condition."[22] These early voices in the Baptist tradition bear witness to an evangelical-sacramental theology in which baptism and the Lord's Supper are understood as "means of grace in the hands of the Holy Spirit."[23] Sacramental signs not only signify grace; they are sources of grace. As Christian philosopher Baron von Hügel put it, "I kiss my child not only because I love it; I kiss it also in order to love it. A religious picture not only expresses my awakened faith; it is a help to my faith's awakening."[24]

Sacraments are also holy ordinances instituted by Christ.[25] Our Lord Jesus Christ commanded his church to baptize (Matt 28:19–20) and celebrate the Supper (1 Cor 11:24–25). These holy sacraments are holy ordinances to keep. They are not our inventions. However, they are not arbitrary commands to obey simply because our Lord commanded. Christ gave these ordinances because they reveal the mystery of the gospel each time we observe them (Rom 16:25–27; Eph 3:6–7, 6:19). He entrusted them to the church. We are servants of Christ and stewards of the mysteries (1 Cor 4:1). Baptism enacts the death, burial, and resurrection of Christ (Rom 6:3–4). The Lord's Supper is a memorial of his death and a proclamation of his coming (1 Cor 11:23–26). However, Jesus did not institute these holy ordinances simply by commanding that we ritually observe them. He instituted them by being the embodiment of God's saving presence. Jesus, the one Word of God, is the sacrament of God's saving presence.[26] Yet Christ is no longer physically with the church. Nevertheless, he continues to be present with us through the Holy Spirit. While it is true that Christ is present to the church through the Spirit, it is also the case that Christ remains incarnate through eternity. He ascended to the right hand of the Father. Christ became incarnate, and he remains incarnate. Yet he is no longer incarnate on earth. He is incarnate in heaven. The Holy Spirit is working in the church, making the incarnate Lord present through word and sacrament. The sacraments, then, as Scottish theologian D. M. Baillie suggested, are extensions of the incarnate presence of Christ to us, though "Christ is present with us, not incarnate in the church, but through the Holy Spirit working in the church by word and sacrament."[27]

The sacraments are holy ordinances and powerful practices, sacred mysteries and faithful duties, signs of presence and seals of promise, gifts of life and means of grace. As has probably become clear by now, the theme of this chapter is not *the sacraments*, the official named rites of the church that mediate God's presence, but *sacramental* practices through which God communicates in holy things. There is a difference between the sacraments and the sacramental, but it is a distinction that is difficult (if not impossible) to sustain. The close connection between the sacraments and sacramental acts is widely recognized. Sacramental actions, like sacraments, signify the promise and presence of God in the life and worship of the church. Martin Luther celebrated two sacraments, but he identified "seven marks of the Body of Christ," which manifest the presence of Christ in his church. Luther's marks included word, baptism, supper, keys, ministry, prayer and praise, and the cross.[28] The Dutch Mennonite Dirk Phillips also named two sacraments, but he described "seven ordinances of the true church," which are the ministry of the word, the sacraments of baptism and supper, washing the feet of the saints, evangelical separation from the world, love for one another, commandment-keeping, and suffering for the gospel.[29] The Separate Baptists in the Old South of colonial

America observed "nine rites" that they held to be central for the ministry and mission of the church. These included baptism, the Lord's Supper, love feasts, laying on of hands, washing feet, anointing the sick, right hand of fellowship, kiss of charity, and devoting children.[30]

I commend seven sacramental practices of preaching, baptizing, breaking bread, washing feet, forgiving, blessing, and anointing through which our lives become connected more fully into the life of God with the people of God. These seven are not an exhaustive set of sacramental practices or an official list of church sacraments. Nevertheless, they are constitutive of the church because they are instruments through which God continues to speak and act as the Spirit makes the risen and ascended Lord present and active in the church. These seven sacramental practices are complex, established, and cooperative activities that form "a life-giving way of life."[31] Each performance involves actions and responses, grace and faith, things and words. They are practices we perform until they become so familiar that we hardly have to think about what we are doing. Repeating them is habit-forming, and these holy habits make holy people. They are holy practices because through them the Holy Spirit mediates the mystery of the gospel.

We speak and hear words. "The word of God for the people of God." "I baptize you in the name of the Father, the Son, and the Holy Spirit." "Take and eat; this is my body." "I wash you that you may share with Christ." "In the name of Jesus Christ, you are forgiven." "The Lord bless you and keep you." "I anoint you in the name of God, who gives you life." In repeating these words, we *say something*, and God *says something* too. More than that, these words *do something*. They are performative. They have an effect or uptake.[32] God acts not because our performance is graceful but because God promises to act when we perform these words: to save those who believe through the preaching of the gospel (1 Cor 1:21), to unite members by baptism into Christ's body (1 Cor 12:13), to mediate fellowship with Christ in the breaking of bread (1 Cor 10:16), to serve others by washing their feet and participating in the ministry of Christ (John 13:8), to forgive and reconcile sinners by hearing their confession and pronouncing words of pardon (Matt 18:15–22), to offer a blessing for God's favor and protection (Num 6:24–26), and to heal and restore sick and suffering souls with the anointing of oil and the laying on of hands (Jas 5:14–16). By performing these words in the church's life and worship, we acquire a memory that we do not have to bring to mind because it becomes second nature to us. These holy practices are ways of knowing the abiding presence of Jesus Christ and nourishing the faith of believers, not by trying to think our way through how Christ is present in these practices. Instead, we develop a shared sense of Christ's presence by gathering in his name, speaking these words, trusting God's promise to act, and discerning the mystery (1 Cor 11:29).

The biblical story of Jacob's ladder has a long and rich tradition in the history of interpretation as a figure of the holy in the ordinary. Jacob falls asleep and dreams of a ladder "set up on the earth" and "reaching to the heaven" with angels "ascending and descending on it" (Gen 28:12). Medieval interpreters commonly identified the ladder connecting heaven and earth with Christ. They read the ladder as a figure of the incarnation—its resting on earth as a reference to Christ's humanity and its reaching to heaven as sign of his divinity. In his commentary on Genesis, Martin Luther followed this line of spiritual interpretation that connected the story of Jacob's ladder with the incarnation of the Word in Christ, but he also understood the ladder as evidence of the visibility of the church through word and sacrament. Glossing his own theological formula on the marks of the church, Luther concluded that wherever the gospel is preached and the sacraments are rightly administered, there is Bethel, the house of God, the gate of heaven, the holy catholic church.[33] John Calvin took a similar approach, describing the ladder as a figure of Christ, "who connects heaven and earth," for "he is the only mediator who reaches from heaven down to earth," and "he is the medium through which the fullness of all celestial blessings flows down to us, and through which we, in turn, ascend to God."[34] Both Calvin and Luther see the christological interpretation as warranted by Christ, who identified himself as the mediator, alluding to his coming crucifixion as Jacob's ladder, when his followers would "see heaven opened and the angels of God ascending and descending upon the Son of Man" (John 1:51). Although Calvin does not connect his view of the sacraments with Jacob's ladder, he suggests that something like it happens, as he describes how, in the Lord's Supper, the Holy Spirit unites us with Christ as we are lifted up into heaven to enjoy Christ's presence and to be spiritually nourished at his table.[35]

John Bunyan and William Blake likewise understand the story of Jacob's ladder as an image of the spiritual connection between heaven and earth. After Christiana and her family come to House Beautiful (a figure for the gathered community), they are taken to a place where they see Jacob's ladder, which, Bunyan tells us, stretches from earth to heaven. There the pilgrims stand gazing, as if in a dreamlike state, at heaven's gate and "feeding their eyes" with the pleasant sight. After having seen the ladder, they are then able to grasp through their spiritual senses and with the gathered community *outside the veil* that which lies *inside the veil*, the Holy of Holies in heaven, where they behold a vision of Christ the mediator and Great High Priest (Heb 6:19–20).[36] Blake's illustration (figure 8) follows Bunyan's description as it depicts Jacob at the base of a winding staircase stretching to heaven, which glows like the sun. Rays of divine glory emanate from the heavenly throne. Human and angelic messengers ascend and descend the staircase, and near sleeping Jacob, two figures bear a tray of food and an urn with drink, suggesting the spiritual nourishment that comes from heaven for weary pilgrims like Jacob who journey by faith.[37] So it is that God invites us to participate, to receive these holy things as gifts, to trust the Word and spirit of promise, to become holy people. Holy things for holy people. Thanks be to God!

Yours in receiving the gift of holy things,

Interpreter

Figure 9

Thus by the Shepherds, Secrets are reveal'd,
Which from all others are kept conceal'd:
Come to the Shepherds, then if you would see
Things deep, things hid, and that mysterious be.[1]

Conclusion

Things Deep, Hid, and Mysterious

Dear Pilgrim:

The story of both parts of *The Pilgrim's Progress* concludes when the pilgrims reach their journey's end and enter the Celestial City. When Christian and Hopeful come to the Delectable Mountains, which they had seen earlier from Palace Beautiful, four shepherds greet them (figure 9).[2] The name of the place is Immanuel's Land, for it lay within sight of the city. The shepherds show the pilgrims many wonders, including a terrifying byway to hell, which is dark and smoky and smelled of brimstone. Afterward, the shepherds lead them to a high hill from which they are able to see the gates of the city through a handheld telescope.[3] The pilgrims learn that before entering the gates of the city, they must pass through the River of Death. None gain entrance without crossing over. When Christian steps into the water, fear overwhelms him. Yet his companion, Hopeful, calls to him, "Be of good cheer, 'Jesus Christ maketh thee whole'" (Acts 9:34, KJV).[4] Hearing those words, Christian cries out, claiming the promise, "When you pass through the waters, I will be with you, and through the rivers, they shall not overwhelm you" (Isa 43:2).[5]

Their final journey brings to mind a popular hymn that came
out of the evangelical revival in Wales:

> When I tread the verge of Jordan,
> Bid my anxious fears subside;
> Death of death, and hell's destruction,
> Land me safe on Canaan's side;
> Songs of praises, songs of praises
> I will ever give to thee.[6]

Taking courage, Christian and Hopeful reach the other
side. When Christiana crosses the river, an angelic entourage
accompanies her to the gates of the city. Her traveling companion and guide, Mr. Great-heart, along with other fellow
pilgrims, follow her.[7]

Early modern Christians like Bunyan were particularly
conscious of death. His contemporary Puritans who journeyed
across the Atlantic to New England commonly engraved the
words *memento mori* ("remember you must die") on their tomb-
stones. No one really knows what it is like to die, although baptism is a dress rehearsal. We are lowered into a watery grave.
We are baptized into Christ's death and raised from the water,
as Christ was raised, that we might walk in the newness of life
(Rom 6:3–4). In the words of the old hymn, we envision the
Promised Land from the waters of baptism as we sing:

> On Jordan's stormy banks I stand,
> And cast a wishful eye,
> To Canaan's fair and happy land,
> Where my possessions lie.[8]

Death is unknown to us on this side of the river. Yet death is
not a mystery. It is an enemy. Death is not natural. It is unnat-
ural. Life is natural. Life is normal. Life is real. Faith is not
about accepting the finality of death. Faith is trusting God to
deliver us from the power of death. This is our hope. This is the

good news: Jesus Christ is the life of the world. As Orthodox
theologian Alexander Schmemann put it,

> Christianity is not reconciliation with death. It is the
> revelation of death, and it reveals death because it is the
> revelation of Life. Christ is this Life. And only if Christ is
> Life is death what Christianity proclaims it to be, namely
> the enemy to be destroyed, and not a "mystery" to be
> explained.[9]

The horror of death is not that it is the end of this life but
rather that it is separation from "the life that really is life"
(1 Tim 6:19), from the life of the world (John 1:4, 17:3).

We face death because we believe in Jesus Christ, who
"suffered under Pontius Pilate, was crucified, died, and was
buried," who "descended to the dead," and "on the third day
he rose again."[10] When I learned to recite the Apostles' Creed
as a child, it stated that Christ "descended into hell." It was
an unfortunate and confusing translation. The original Latin
words *ad inferna* mean something like "to the lower regions"
not "into hell." The word *inferno* is more closely associated in
biblical terms with *sheol*, the shadowy realm of the dead, not
gehenna, a place of eternal torment and punishment, but it is
probably better to render it simply as "the grave" or "the dead."
The newer translation, "descended to the dead," is a better
rendering of the Latin phrase. This more accurate translation,
however, has not settled the matter of its interpretation.[11] Some
suggest that the phrase repeats the theme of the previous line,
emphasizing the reality of Jesus's death and burial.[12] Others
read it as an allusion to the apocryphal story of Christ's harrowing raid on hell in which he battled with satanic forces
to deliver the righteous held captive since the foundation of
the world.[13] Still others understand it as a statement of the
physical and spiritual torment that Christ suffered, taking on

the depth of the human condition and experiencing a sense of abandonment by the Father.[14] Another way of understanding the descent is to see it as an affirmation that Christ experienced death as all humans do but was raised from the dead by the power of the Spirit, whereby he proclaimed victory to the dead who were imprisoned in the grave by the powers of death (1 Pet 3:19; Rom 1:4).[15] There is a sense in which all four interpretations convey something important about why the doctrine of Christ's descent was included in the creed and has persisted as a belief in the church.

Several years ago, I visited the Elmina Slave Castle in Cape Coast, Ghana, where, for centuries, large numbers of African captives were imprisoned before being transported by the middle passage across the Atlantic to North America and the Caribbean, at which point they were sold into slavery. The slave castle was the site of the first Christian chapel in Ghana. Portuguese Catholic slave merchants built it in the fifteenth century. When the Dutch seized the castle and took over the slave trade in the seventeenth century, they built a Protestant church on the site. Hidden deep beneath the churches were dungeons that housed prisoners awaiting transport. There was one chamber for men and another for women. Each could accommodate hundreds of captives at a time, crowded close together. The prisoners were subjected to unbelievably cruel and inhumane conditions. There were no windows or toilets. It was dark and dank. It was sweltering in the heat, and the stench must have been intolerable. It is hard to imagine how human beings could survive such an environment. Eventually, the prisoners were loaded into the ships that would bear them into a lifetime of slavery. As they made their way to the vessels, they passed through the "door of no return." It was the last thing they saw before entering what can only be described as hell on earth. It is not unlike Dante's account of the inscription at the entrance of hell, which read, "Abandon all hope ye who enter here."[16] Many did abandon hope. It is hard to imagine why they would not. It is even harder to imagine how slave traders could claim to follow the same Jesus Christ who said, "If you continue in my word, you are truly my disciples, and you will know the truth, and the truth will make you free" (John 8:31–32). The Africans were not free, imprisoned within walls of stone and held by shackles of iron. Yet the Europeans were held in bondage of another sort. For the liberating word of the gospel did not, indeed could not, reach the souls of those who preyed upon and prayed over Black bodies. Can the light of hope ever penetrate such deep darkness?

Between 1954 and 1964, Karl Barth preached often at the penitentiary in Basel, Switzerland.[17] We might ask why such a distinguished theologian continued to preach to those forcibly alienated from church and society. In a letter dated August 1, 1955, Barth wrote, "I really like to go there, feel somehow in solidarity with these men, am moved as I enthusiastically listen to them."[18] It becomes clear from reading these sermons that Barth's experience in prison ministry led him to understand something of what Jesus did in preaching to the spirits in prison when he descended to the dead (1 Pet 3:19). There among prisoners, Barth rediscovered what it means to proclaim "deliverance to the captives" (Luke 4:18, KJV). In the sermon "All!" Barth reflects on the text: "For God has imprisoned all in disobedience so that he may be merciful to all" (Rom 11:32). He announces that we must start with the fact that "God had mercy and will have mercy on all."[19] This is good news. We do not deserve God's mercy. By right, God should say no to all, but in Jesus Christ, God says yes, and God's "yes" is unequivocal, never to be reversed by a no. God's Word spoken in Jesus Christ is mercy for all. Yet God's mercy is a result of the fact that God has made all humanity prisoners of disobedience. All have disobeyed God and are imprisoned behind walls from which there is no escape. To disobey God, Barth says, means we reserve the right to go our own ways, to "affirm in our innermost hearts and with our outward life that there is no God."[20] Yet Jesus Christ was obedient unto death. He did not resist or rebel against God's will. He submitted to it. Because he bore the no of God's rejection for all, in him, God's promises are "yes" and "amen" (2 Cor 1:20).

This, Barth announces, is the message of Easter: "Death— but life!"[21] Its sound resonates throughout the Christian Scriptures. Jesus declared, "Very truly, I tell you, anyone who hears my word and believes him who sent me has eternal life and does not come under judgment but has passed from death to life" (John 5:24). The apostle Paul also proclaimed that our Savior Jesus Christ "abolished death and brought life and immortality to light through the gospel" (2 Tim 1:10). However, the key text Barth chose for this sermon states, "For the wages of sin is death, but the free gift of God is eternal life in Christ Jesus our Lord" (Rom 6:23). Jesus made our story his own. He took our sin on himself. He accepted the wages for our sin. He suffered, was crucified, died, and was buried. He descended into death. Easter begins there, in the tomb, where we all lay with him. The wages of sin were paid on Easter morning. We died with him on the cross. Our no struck him, who was without sin, who did not deserve death. Yet that was not the end of the story. God's gift is eternal life. With the resurrection of Jesus from the dead, God's gift of eternal life came into the world. His story is now our story. Just as God said in creation, "Let there be light" (Gen 1:3), in the new creation, "the light shines in the darkness, and the darkness did not overtake it" (John 1:5). Christ's descent to the dead, then, becomes discernible, not in the darkness of the cross but in the light of the resurrection.

Because God was with Jesus when he suffered the agony of Gethsemane on Maundy Thursday, the torment of the cross on Good Friday, and the abandonment of the grave on Holy Saturday, we are assured that God is with us when we walk through the valley of the shadow of death (Ps 23:4, KJV). Because he accepted the sentence that was ours, God joined Christ's life with ours, and because God was in Christ as he suffered punishment for us, we know that God is present with us in our suffering. In his commentary on Psalm 22, Martin Luther noted that Christ experienced death, which is the punishment of sin, but Luther indicated that Christ suffered more than death. He underwent "the dread and horror of a distressed conscience, which feels eternal wrath, and feels as if it were utterly forsaken to all eternity and cast off from the face of God." Christ faced the reality of what it means "to be killed and damned, or to be in death and hell." Luther argued that Christ had the same consciousness as the damned, adding, "He was tempted in all points like as we are, yet without sin" (Heb 4:15).[22] John Calvin went further, proposing that Christ's descent to the dead signifies not so much the location of his suffering but the condition of one "whom God has condemned and doomed to destruction."[23] Calvin further stated that Christ descended to the grave and experienced not simply the death of his body but the death of his soul, which means he felt the despair and desolation of abandonment by God, suffering "the terrible torments of a condemned and forsaken man."[24] Yet even though he felt abandoned by God, he did not waver in his trust in the goodness of God, and "even though he suffered beyond measure, he did not cease to call [God] his God, by whom he cried out that he had been forsaken."[25] Calvin concluded, "The only thing which

can temper the bitterness of [death's] agonies is to know that
God is our Father, and that we have Christ for our leader and
companion."[26]

Christ descended to the dead to bring us to life: "We
were buried with him by baptism into death, so that, just as
Christ was raised from the dead by the glory of the Father, so
we also might walk in newness of life" (Rom 6:4). Baptism,
then, saves us—"not as a removal of dirt from the body but
as an appeal to God for a good conscience, through the resurrection of Jesus Christ, who has gone into heaven and is at
the right hand of God, with angels, authorities, and powers
made subject to him" (1 Pet 3:21–22). Jesus bore the penalty
and punishment of our sin. He took the pain and agony of
our traumatic existence with him into the grave. The fullness of our lives is now "hidden with Christ in God" (Col
3:3). As the Heidelberg Catechism affirms, we have assurance
"during attacks of deepest dread and temptation that Christ
[our] Lord, by suffering unspeakable anguish, pain, and terror
of soul, on the cross but also earlier, has delivered [us] from
hellish anguish and torment."[27] Here it becomes clearer what
Christ's descent into death means for those who struggle in
their faith journey, especially those who survive physical, psy-
chological, or spiritual trauma. Though Christ was the sinless
Son, he felt alienated from the Father, expressing his distress
in prayers of lamentation. In our pain and grief, we can follow
Christ's example of lament by expressing our feelings of alien-
ation from and anger toward God. In doing so, we can rest in
the confidence that doubt and struggle are not necessarily the
opposite of faith but can be an appropriate response to God
and an expression of Christian faithfulness. By joining with
Jesus in addressing God with our sense of forsakenness, we
discover not only the catharsis of our emotions. We experience
communion with the Father and begin the journey of healing
and reconciliation.[28]

As I write this final letter, I have been reading a book by a former student and fellow minister. It tells his story about how he found joy on death row.[29] It is a remarkable account of his ministry among prisoners sentenced to death for horrific crimes. Each one had perpetrated violence on others and was pronounced guilty for their offenses, but all had also been subjected to injustice and often to violence by a criminal justice system whose only answer to violence is retribution and punishment. My friend expected to encounter individuals facing a bitter and miserable existence as they awaited their appointed deaths. Instead, he surprisingly found people filled with joy. In their conversations, he sought to discover the source of their strength. I also learned from reading that my friend had lost his joy. Many years earlier, when he was a young adult, his sister had murdered his father and attempted to kill his mother. The trauma of that event resulted in his sister's confinement to a psychiatric hospital. Unable to live with the burden of guilt and shame that followed, his family members became alienated from one another. My friend describes how for decades he lived a defeated life, devoid of joy, until he found joy in Christ on death row. However, if we consider that Christ descended to the dead, where he preached to the spirits in prison (1 Pet 3:19), perhaps finding joy among prisoners should not be as surprising as we might think. For Christ descended to death row before us. As one Christian theologian observed, "If Jesus took on the sins of the world and suffered the ultimate judgment of guilt and defeat, then I am convinced that he found camaraderie and understanding among the prisoners in hell," adding, "His descent was the first step toward his resurrection and our rehabilitation."[30]

Christ descended to the dead. He has already gone to the scary place before us so that we do not have to go there alone. He has turned the dark place into a place of light because we trust him, as the Psalmist declares,

O Lord, you brought up my soul from Sheol,
    restored me to life from among those gone down
        to the Pit.
Sing praises to the Lord, O you his faithful ones,
    and give thanks to his holy name.
For his anger is but for a moment;
    his favor is for a lifetime.
Weeping may linger for the night,
    but joy comes with the morning. (Ps 30:3–5)

So we call out to the One who is our help:

When the darkness appears,
And the night draws near,
And the day is past and gone.
At the river I stand,
Guide my feet, hold my hand,
Take my hand precious Lord,
Lead me home.[31]

Death is an unknown to us. Yet death is not a mystery. Death is an enemy. As we face death, we follow Jesus, who went to the grave with the words: "You will not abandon my soul to Hades" (Acts 2:27). Following him, we offer up our prayers with tears to the One who alone can save us from death. We trust to be heard in reverent submission, and we seek to learn obedience in our suffering that we might go on to perfection and share in eternal salvation through Jesus Christ our Lord (Heb 5:7–10). For the final mystery, as Scripture promises, is not that "it is appointed for mortals to die once and after that the judgment" (Heb 9:27) but that "we will all be changed, in a moment, in the twinkling of an eye, at the last trumpet" (1 Cor 15:51–52). Yes and amen!

Yours in discerning the mystery,
Interpreter

Illustrations

Notes

PREFACE

1 Peter Wehner, "The Evangelical Church Is Breaking Apart,"
   The *Atlantic*, October 24, 2021, accessed August 29, 2022,
   https://www.theatlantic.com/ideas/archive/2021/10/
   evangelical-trump-christians-politics/620469.

2 J. I. Packer and Gary A. Parrett, *Grounded in the Gospel: Building Believers the Old-Fashioned Way* (Grand Rapids, MI: Baker,
   2010), 184.

3 Packer and Parrett, *Grounded in the Gospel*, 10–11.

4 "Constitution on the Sacred Liturgy," *Sacrosanctum Concilium*
   (December 4, 1963), §64, in *Vatican Council II*, vol. 1, *The Con-
   ciliar and Postconciliar Documents*, rev. ed., ed. Austin Flannery
   (Northport, NY: Costello Publishing Company, 2004), 21.

5 Catholic Church, *Rite of Christian Initiation of Adults*, study ed.
   (Chicago: Liturgy Training, 1988); and Thomas H. Morris, *The
   RCIA: Transforming the Church* (New York: Paulist Press, 1997).

6 Curtis W. Freeman, *Pilgrim Letters: Instruction in the Basic Teaching of Christ* (Minneapolis: Fortress Press, 2021).

7 The Institute for the Recovery of Christian Catechesis, https://
   www.catechesisrenewal.com/.

8 Ryan Burge, *The Nones: Where They Came From, Who They
   Are, and Where They Are Going* (Minneapolis: Fortress, 2021),

1–6. The 2018 General Social Survey that Burge refers to in the book noted the nones as 23.7 percent of the US population. The percentage is increasing, and Burge reported that it is about 30 percent. Jeff Brumley, "Ryan Burge Sifts the Data to Paint an Evolving Portrait of the 'Nones,'" *Baptist News Global,* April 1, 2021, accessed July 31, 2022, https://baptistnews.com/article/ryan-burge-sifts-the-data-to-paint-an-evolving-portrait-of-the-nones/#.YubGNYTMKUk.

9 James Wm. McClendon Jr., *Ethics: Systematic Theology, Volume I,* rev. ed. (Waco, TX: Baylor University Press, 2012), 17.

10 Alan Kreider, *The Change of Conversion and the Origin of Christendom* (Harrisburg, PA: Trinity Press, 1999), xv.

11 Robert E. Webber, *Ancient-Future Faith: Rethinking Evangelicalism for a Postmodern World* (Grand Rapids, MI: Baker, 1999), 7.

12 It would be a mistake to portray this call to reexamine the past in order to face the future as merely primitivism or restorationism in disguise. Stepping back is crucial to going forward in the hermeneutical movement of critical naïveté, as described by Paul Ricoeur, *The Symbolism of Evil* (Boston: Beacon, 1967), 349. In this book, I retrieve theological grammar from the past to reenvision ecclesial practice for the future. In this sense, I am following the pattern of earlier theologians like Yves Congar and Henri De Lubac, who exemplified theology as a dynamic process that included both development (*ressourcement*) and reformulation (*aggiornamento*). Yves Congar, *Divided Christendom* (London: G. Bles, 1939); Henri de Lubac, *The Mystery of the Supernatural* (London: G. Chapman, 1967); Lubac, *Medieval Exegesis: The Four Senses of Scripture*, 3 vols., trans. Mark Sebanc and E. M. Macierowski (Grand Rapids, MI: Eerdmans, 1998–2009). Karl Barth is the great example of a Protestant theology of constructive retrieval that resources traditional theological categories for contemporary purposes. Karl Barth, *Church Dogmatics*, trans. G. W. Bromiley et al. (Edinburgh: T & T Clark, 1956–1969). Cornell West, Willie James Jennings, and Sarah Coakley are three contemporary theologians who have explored this pattern of retrieval and revision with a special attention to matters of race and gender. Cornell West, *Prophesy Deliverance! An Afro-American Revolutionary Christianity* (Philadelphia: Westminster,

1982); Willie James Jennings, *The Christian Imagination: Theology and the Origins of Race* (New Haven, CT: Yale University Press, 2010); Sarah Coakley, *Powers and Submissions: Spirituality, Philosophy, and Gender* (Oxford: Blackwell, 2002); and Coakley, *God, Sexuality and the Self: An Essay 'On The Trinity'* (Cambridge, UK: Cambridge University Press, 2013). Theological renewal demands a sophisticated hermeneutic of reflection, which accounts for a process of development and reformulation and includes both retrieval and revision. For more on this approach, see Darren Sarisky, ed., *Theologies of Retrieval: An Exploration and Appraisal* (New York: Bloomsbury T & T Clark, 2017).

13 Loren B. Mead, *The Once and Future Church: Reinventing the Congregation for a New Mission Frontier* (Washington, DC: Alban, 1991).

14 Curtis W. Freeman, *Undomesticated Dissent: Democracy and the Public Virtue of Religious Nonconformity* (Waco, TX: Baylor University Press, 2017), 223–24. See also James Wm. McClendon Jr., *Witness: Systematic Theology, Volume III* (Waco, TX: Baylor University Press, 2012), 345–83.

15 Tertullian, "Apology," trans. S. Thelwall, in *The Ante-Nicene Fathers* (Grand Rapids, MI: Eerdmans, 1978), 3:32.

16 McClendon, *Ethics*, 30; James Wm. McClendon Jr., *Doctrine: Systematic Theology, Volume II* (Waco, TX: Baylor University Press, 2012), 45–46.

17 Stanley Hauerwas, *The Work of Theology* (Grand Rapids, MI: Eerdmans, 2015), 26–29.

18 Maxwell E. Johnson, *Rites of Christian Initiation: Their Evolution and Interpretation*, 2nd ed. (Collegeville, MI: Liturgical Press, 2007), xviii.

19 Hippolytus, *The Apostolic Tradition*, xvi–xxxviii, in Gregory Dix and Henry Chadwick, ed., *The Treatise on the Apostolic Tradition of St. Hippolytus of Rome*, 2nd rev. ed. (London: Alban Press, 1992), 23–72.

20 Robert E. Webber, *Journey to Jesus: The Worship, Evangelism, and Nurture Mission of the Church* (Nashville: Abingdon, 2001), 11–15; Webber, *Ancient-Future Evangelism: Making Your Church a Faith-Forming Community* (Grand Rapids, MI: Baker, 2003), 23–25.

21 *Egeria's Travels to the Holy Land*, §§45–47, rev. ed. (Jerusalem: Ariel Publishing, 1981), 143–46.

22 Cyril of Jerusalem, "Catechetical Lectures," 19–23, trans. Edwin Hamilton Gifford, in *The Nicene and Post-Nicene Fathers* (Grand Rapids, MI: Eerdmans, 1978), 7:144–57.

23 Frank C. Senn, *A Stewardship of the Mysteries* (Mahwah, NJ: Paulist Press, 1999), 1–4.

24 Augustine, *City of God*, 15.20, trans. Henry Bettenson (New York: Penguin, 1984), 630.

25 Eugene H. Peterson, *A Long Obedience in the Same Direction: Discipleship in an Instant Society* (Downers Grove, IL: InterVarsity Press, 1980).

26 "The Orthodox Creed," 19, in William L. Lumpkin, *Baptist Confessions of Faith*, rev. ed. (Valley Forge, PA: Judson, 1969), 311–12.

27 Thomas M. Finn, *Early Christian Baptism and the Catechumenate: West and East Syria*, Message of the Fathers of the Church, vol. 5 (Collegeville, MN: The Liturgical Press, 1992), 5.

28 David B. Burrell, *Friendship and Ways to Truth* (Notre Dame, IN: University of Notre Dame Press, 2000), 2.

INTRODUCTION: THE MYSTERY HIDDEN THROUGH THE AGES

1 John Bunyan, *The Pilgrim's Progress*, second part, ed. N. H. Keeble (New York: Oxford 1984), 147.

2 Arthur Conan Doyle, *The Sign of Four* (London: Spencer Blackett, 1890), 93. Emphasis in the original.

3 Gabriel Marcel, *Being and Having*, trans. Katharine Farrer (Westminster: Dacre Press, 1949), 117.

4 Jeff Conklin, "Wicked Problems and Social Complexity," in *Dialogue Mapping: Building Shared Understanding of Wicked Problems* (Chichester: Wiley, 2006), 3–40. Conklin names six characteristics of wicked problems: they are not understood until there is a developed solution, there is no stopping rule, there are no right or wrong solutions, every wicked problem is unique, every solution is a "one-shot operation," and there are no alternative solutions.

5 Gordon D. Kaufman, *God the Problem* (Cambridge, MA: Harvard University Press, 1972), 3–16.

6 Simone Weil, "Spiritual Autobiography," in *Waiting for God*, trans. Emma Craufurd (New York: HarperCollins, 1973), 61–83, esp. 62 and 68.

7 David B. Burrell, *Aquinas: God and Action*, 3rd ed., ed. Mary Budde Ragan (Eugene, OR: Wipf and Stock, 2016); David B. Burrell, *Friendship and Ways to Truth* (Notre Dame, IN: University of Notre Dame Press, 2000), 100–107; Stephen Mulhall, *The Great Riddle: Wittgenstein and Nonsense, Theology and Philosophy* (Oxford: Oxford University Press, 2015), 54–55.

8 Michael J. Buckley, *At the Origins of Modern Atheism* (New Haven, CT: Yale University Press, 1990), 346.

9 Charles Hartshorne, *The Divine Relativity: A Social Conception of God* (New Haven, CT: Yale University Press, 1948), 1.

10 Anselm, "Proslogion," 2, in *The Prayers and Meditations of Saint Anselm*, trans. Benedicta Ward (New York: Penguin, 1973), 244.

11 Theophilus of Antioch, "First Book to Autolycus," 5, quoted in Oliver Clément, *The Roots of Christian Mysticism*, 2nd ed. (Hyde Park, NY: New City Press, 2019), 26.

12 Eberhard Jüngel, *God as the Mystery of the World*, trans. Darrell L. Guder (London: Bloomsbury, 1983), 250–54.

13 Mulhall, *The Great Riddle*, 8–11.

14 Denys Turner, *The Darkness of God: Negativity in Christian Mysticism* (Cambridge, UK: Cambridge University Press, 1995), 19–20.

15 *The Book of Common Prayer*, according to the use of the Episcopal Church (New York: Church Publishing, 2007), 323.

16 George I. Mavrodes, "Some Puzzles Concerning Omnipotence," *Philosophical Review* 72, no. 2 (April 1963): 221–223.

17 Nicholas Lash, *Easter in Ordinary: Reflections on Human Experience and the Knowledge of God* (Charlottesville: University of Virginia Press, 1988), 49.

18 Another reading of this verse might be "It is he that made us, and we are his."

19 J. I. Packer, *Knowing God* (Downers Grove, IL: InterVarsity, 1973), 25–26.

20 Friedrich Gogarten, *Von Glauben und Offenbarung, Vier Vor-träge* (Jena: Eugen Diederichs, 1923), 11. Quoted in Brand Blanshard, *Reason and Belief* (London: George Allen & Unwin, 1974), 291.

21 Karl Barth, *Church Dogmatics*, II/1, trans. T. H. L. Parker, W. B. Johnston, Harold Knight, and J. L. M. Haire (Edinburgh: T & T Clark, 1957), 179.

22 James K. A. Smith, *You Are What You Love: The Spiritual Power of Habit* (Grand Rapids, MI: Brazos, 2016), 3–9.

23 Gregory of Nyssa, *The Life of Moses*, II. 162, trans. Abraham J. Malherbe and Everett Ferguson (New York: Paulist Press, 1978), 94.

24 Gregory of Nyssa, *The Life of Moses*, II. 223, 112–13.

25 Andrew Louth, *Discerning the Mystery: An Essay on the Nature of Theology* (Oxford: Clarendon Press, 1983), 144–47.

26 William Cowper, "God Moves in a Mysterious Way," in *Olney Hymns,* in Three Parts, by Cowper and John Newton, Book III 15 (New York: T. Nelson and Sons, 1855), 262–63.

27 Cyril of Jerusalem, "The Catechetical Lectures," Procatechesis, 12 and Lecture VI. 29, in *The Nicene and Post-Nicene Fathers*, second series, trans. Philip Schaff and Henry Wace (Grand Rapids, MI: Eerdmans, 1978), 7:4, 42.

28 "Los Enters the Door of Death," *Jerusalem,* plate 1. Frontispiece, copy E, in *William Blake the Complete Illuminated Books* (New York: Thames & Hudson, 2001), 298.

29 William Blake, "Jerusalem: The Emanation of the Giant Albion," plate 45 [31], line 3, in *The Poetry and Prose of William Blake*, ed. David V. Erdman (New York: Doubleday, 1970), 192.

MYSTERY 1 ONE WORD: JESUS CHRIST

1 Bunyan, *The Pilgrim's Progress*, 240.

2 "Chalcedon's Definition of Faith," trans. and ed. R. A. Norris, Jr. in *The Christological Controversy* (Philadelphia: Fortress Press, 1980), 159.

3 Karl Barth, *Church Dogmatics*, I/1, trans. G. W. Bromiley (Edinburgh: T & T Clark, 1957), 88–124.

4 Ignatius of Antioch, "Letter to the Magnesians," 8.2, in *The Early Christian Fathers*, trans. and ed. Cyril C. Richardson (New York: Collier Books, 1970), 96.

5 Maximus the Confessor, "Ambigua," in Oliver Clément, *The Roots of Christian Mysticism*, 2nd ed. (Hyde Park, NY: New City Press, 2019), 38.

6 Martin Luther, *The Bondage of the Will*, trans. Philip S. Watson, in *Luther's Works* (Philadelphia: Fortress, 1972), 33:138–44.

7 Luther, "Heidelberg Disputation," trans. Harold J. Grimm, in *Luther's Works* (Philadelphia, PA: Fortress, 1957), 31:52–53.

8 "Chalcedon's Definition of Faith," 159.

9 Karl Barth, *Church Dogmatics*, IV/2, ed. G. W. Bromiley and T. F. Torrance (Edinburgh: T. & T. Clark, 1958), 49–60; Thomas F. Torrence, *Incarnation: The Person and Life of Christ*, ed. Robert T. Walker (Downers Grove, IL: InterVarsity, 2008), 84, 105. This twofold way of describing the humanity of Christ is crucial to the Chalcedonian formula because it indicates what he shares with all humans (*anhypostasia*) and what he shares with God (*enhypostasia*).

10 "Articles of Religion of the New Connexion," 3, in William L. Lumpkin, ed., *Baptist Confessions of Faith*, rev. ed. (Valley Forge, PA: Judson Press, 1969), 343.

11 Jaroslav Pelikan and Valerie Hotchkiss, eds. *Creeds and Confession of Faith in the Christian Tradition*, 4 vols. (New Haven, CT: Yale University Press, 2004), 1:162–63.

12 D. M. Baillie, *God Was in Christ: An Essay on Incarnation and Atonement* (New York: Scribners, 1948), 108–9.

13 McClendon, *Doctrine*, 274–79.

14 McClendon, *Doctrine*, 272.

15 Robert Barron, *The Priority of Christ: Toward a Postliberal Catholicism* (Grand Rapids, MI: Brazos Press, 2007), 65–66; Terrence W. Tilley, *The Disciples' Jesus: Christology as Reconciling Practice* (Maryknoll, NY: Orbis Books, 2008), 35–36; David H. Kelsey *Proving Doctrine: The Uses of Scripture in Modern Theology* (Harrisburg, PA: Trinity Press, 1999), 39–50. Kelsey suggests that a kind of two-narratives approach is at work in the Christology of Karl Barth's treatment of "the Royal Man" in *Church Dogmatics*, IV/2, §64.3, 154–264.

16   Augustine, "On Rebuke and Grace," 33, trans. Peter Holmes and
      Robert Ernest Wallis, and rev. Benjamin B. Warfield, in *The
      Nicene and Post Nicene Fathers* (Grand Rapids, MI: Eerdmans,
      1971), 5:485; Augustine, *City of God*, 22.30, 1089.

17   Robert W. Jenson, *Systematic Theology, Volume 1: The Triune God*
      (New York: Oxford, 1997), 134–37. Jenson draws on the trini-
      tarian account of Maximus the Confessor in his *Ambigua*.

18   Karl Barth, *Church Dogmatics*, IV.1 §§57–58 (Edinburgh: T &
      T Clark, 1956), 3–154.

19   William Blake, "Christ Nailed to the Cross: The Third Hour" was
      part of a collection on the passion of Christ commissioned for
      Thomas Butts in 1799. Another drawing in the same collection,
      The Crucifixion: Behold Thy Mother, depicts Mary and John at the
      foot of the cross. Martin Butlin, *William Blake 1757–1827*, Tate
      Gallery Collections, V (London: The Tate Gallery, 1990).

20   Victoria J. Barnett, "German Protestantism and the Challenges
      of National Socialism," *American Baptist Quarterly* 37, no. 4
      (Winter 2014): 388–404.

21   Arthur C. Cochrane, *The Church's Confessions under Hitler* (Phil-
      adelphia: Westminster Press, 1962), 239.

22   James Wm. McClendon Jr., "Atonement, Discipleship and Free-
      dom," *Baptist Student* 44 (November 1964): 55.

MYSTERY 2 TWO TESTAMENTS: CHRISTIAN SCRIPTURE

1   Bunyan, *The Pilgrim's Progress*, 249.

2   Konrad Schmid and Jens Schröter, *The Making of the Bible: From
     the First Fragments to Sacred Scripture*, trans. Peter Lewis (Cam-
     bridge, MA: Belknap Press, 2021), 1–42.

3   R. Kendall Soulen, *The God of Israel and Christian Theology*
     (Minneapolis: Fortress, 1996), ix–xii; Michael Goldberg, *Jews
     and Christians Getting Our Stories Straight: The Exodus and the
     Passion-Resurrection* (Nashville: Abingdon, 1985), 8.

4   Christopher R. Seitz, *The Character of Christian Scripture: The
     Significance of a Two-Testament Bible* (Grand Rapids, MI: Baker
     Academic, 2011), 17–25.

5 The Second Helvitic Confession, 1, in Presbyterian Church
   (USA), *Book of Confessions*, rev. study ed. (Louisville, KY: West-
   minster/John Knox Press, 2017), 125.

6 Anna Bartlett Warner, "Jesus Loves Me," in *Say and Seal*, 2 vols.
   (Philadelphia: Lippincott, 1880), 115.

7 *The Westminster Shorter Catechism*, Q.2, in Presbyterian Church
   (USA), *Book of Confessions*, rev. study ed. (Louisville, KY: West-
   minster/John Knox Press, 2017), 269.

8 Homer L. Grice, *The Daily Vacation Bible School Guide* (Nashville: Southern Baptist Sunday School Board, 1926), 243. Grice
   was the first secretary of the Vacation Bible School Department
   of the Southern Baptist Sunday School Board and composed the
   pledge based on Psalm 119:105 and 11.

9 W. R. Owens, "Bunyan and the Bible," in *The Cambridge Companion to Bunyan*, ed. Anne Dunan-Page (New York: Cambridge
   University Press, 2010), 39–50.

10 Bunyan, *The Pilgrim's Progress*, 8–9.

11 Bunyan draws from his own experience of grace in his description of Christian's struggle to read the Bible, *Grace Abounding
   to the Chief of Sinners*, §§29–39, ed. W. R. Owens (New York:
   Penguin, 1987), 12–14.

12 Bunyan, *The Pilgrim's Progress*, 187.

13 Bunyan, *The Pilgrim's Progress*, 221.

14 Bunyan, *The Pilgrim's Progress*, 240.

15 Bunyan, *The Pilgrim's Progress*, 243.

16 Bunyan, *The Pilgrim's Progress*, 250.

17 Bunyan, *The Pilgrim's Progress*, 249.

18 Bunyan, *Grace Abounding*, §§324–25; Owens, "Bunyan and the
   Bible," 79.

19 F. F. Bruce, *The Books and the Parchments*, rev. ed. (Old Tappan,
   NJ: Fleming H. Revell, 1963), 70–71.

20 Karl Barth, *Church Dogmatics*, I/1, trans. G. W. Bromiley (Edin-
   burgh: T. & T. Clark, 1957), 107; Stephen B. Chapman, "What
   Are We Reading? Canonicity and the Old Testament," *Word and
   World* 29, no. 4 (Fall 2009): 347.

21 Brevard S. Childs, *Biblical Theology of the Old and New Testaments* (Minneapolis: Fortress, 1992), 722.

22   J. Louis Martyn, *Galatians*, in *The Anchor Yale Bible*, 33A (New Haven, CT: Yale University Press, 1997), 336–352.

23   Bernard Green, *European Baptists and the Third Reich* (Didcot: Baptist Historical Society, 1997).

24   "An Account of Our Faith," art. V, in G. Keith Parker, *Baptists in Europe: History and Confessions of Faith* (Nashville: Broadman, 1982), 62. Emphasis added.

25   *Rechenschaft vom Glauben*, 5, accessed August 7, 2019, https://www.baptisten.de/fileadmin/bgs/media/dokumente/Rechenschaft_vom_Glauben_-_Stand_31.05.2019.pdf. An unauthorized English translation is available on the German Baptist Union website, accessed August 7, 2019, https://www.baptisten.de/fileadmin/bgs/media/dokumente/English-Version_The-people-of-Israel-and-the-church-of-Jesus-Christ.pdf.

26   Justin Martyr, "Dialogue with Trypho," 119, 123, and 135, trans. Marcus Dods and George Reith, in *The Ante-Nicene Fathers*, ed. Alexander Roberts, James Donaldson, and A. Cleveland Coxe (Grand Rapids, MI: Eerdmans, 1950), 1:258–59, 261, and 267.

27   Soulen, *The God of Israel and Christian Theology*, 1–21.

28   George A. Lindbeck, *The Church in a Postliberal Age*, ed. James J. Buckley (Grand Rapids, MI: Eerdmans, 2002), 157.

29   Augustine, "On the Spirit and the Letter," 27, trans. Benjamin B. Warfield, in *The Nicene and Post-Nicene Fathers* (Grand Rapids, MI: Eerdmans, 1978), 5:95.

30   William Blake, "Christ in the Sepulchre, Guarded by Angels," 1805, in the Victoria and Albert Museum, London.

31   Karl Barth, *Church Dogmatics*, I/2, trans. G. T. Thomson and Harold Knight (Edinburgh: T. & T. Clark, 1956), 101–21, 481–85.

MYSTERY 3 THREE PERSONS: THE HOLY TRINITY

1   Bunyan, *The Pilgrim's Progress*, 185.

2   James Weldon Johnson, *God's Trombones* (New York: Penguin Books, 1976), 4–5.

3   "Nuns on the Run," directed by Jonathan Lynn, March 30, 1990, UK: HandMade Films, 1990, Video.

4   Harry Emerson Fosdick, *Dear Mr. Brown: Letters to a Person Perplexed about Religion* (New York: Harper and Row, 1961), 120.

5   Augustine, "On the Trinity," 5.9.10, trans. W. G. T. Shedd, in
    The Nicene and Post-Nicene Fathers (Grand Rapids, MI: Eerd-
    mans, 1978), 3:92.

6   Jacobus de Voragine, *The Golden Legend or Lives of the Saints*,
    trans. William Caxton, in *Temple Classics*, ed. F. S. Ellis, 7 vols.
    (London: J. M. Dent and Co., 1900), 5:23.

7   Brian Wren, *What Language Shall I Borrow?: God-Talk in Wor-
    ship: A Male Response to Feminist Theology* (New York: Crossroad,
    1990), 55.

8   Janet Martin Soskice, *The Kindness of God: Metaphor, Gender,
    and Religious Language* (New York: Oxford, 2007), 117.

9   Elizabeth A. Johnson, *She Who Is: The Mystery of God in Feminist
    Theological Discourse* (New York: Crossroad, 1992), 42–57.

10 Gregory of Nazianzus, "Oration," 3:16, in *The Nicene and Post-
    Nicene Fathers*, second series, trans. Charles Gordon Browne and
    James Edward Swallow (Grand Rapids, MI: Eerdmans, 1976),
    7:307.

11 David C. Steinmetz, "Inclusive Language and the Trinity," in
    Memory and Mission: Theological Reflections on the Christian Past
    (Nashville: Abingdon, 1988), 126–34; Ted Peters, *God as Trin-
    ity: Relationality and Temporality in Divine Life* (Louisville, KY:
    Westminster/John Knox, 1993), 46.

12 Ruth C. Duck, *Gender and the Name of God: The Trinitar-
    ian Baptismal Formula* (New York: Pilgrim Press, 1991),
    163–66; James F. Kay, "In Whose Name?: Feminism and the
    Trinitarian Baptismal Formula," *Theology Today* 9, no. 4 (Jan-
    uary 1993): 531; Paula Herbert, "Nonsexist Language," *Wash-
    ington Post,* May 28, 1983, accessed September 13, 2022,
    https://www.washingtonpost.com/archive/local/1983/05/28/
    nonsexist-language/4cbb8cce-76b3–4fae-8070–3aac1ed3e9aa/.

13 Kathryn Greene-McCreight, "When I Say God, I Mean Father,
    Son and Holy Spirit: On the Ecumenical Baptismal Formula," *Pro
    Ecclesia* 6, no. 3 (Summer 1997): 289–308; Greene-McCreight,
    "Feminist Liturgical Trinities and a Generous Orthodoxy," in
    The Place of Christ in Liturgical Prayer, ed. Brian D. Spinks (Col-
    legeville, MN: Liturgical Press, 2008), 360–78.

14 Janet Martin Soskice, *Metaphor and Religious Language* (New
    York: Clarendon Press, 1985), 15.

15   Soskice, *The Kindness of God*, 66–83.

16   Martin Buber, *I and Thou*, trans. Walter Kaufmann (New York: Touchstone, 1970), 123.

17   Athanasius, "Against the Arians," 3.27.36, in *The Nicene and Post-Nicene Fathers*, second series, trans. John Henry Newman and Archibald Robertson (Grand Rapids, MI: Eerdmans, 1978), 4:413. The Trinitarian grammatical principle is a paraphrase of the Athanasian *leitmotif*.

18   Gregory of Nazianzus, "Oration," 38.8, in *The Nicene and Post-Nicene Fathers*, second series, 7:347.

19   Thomas Jefferson, "Doctrines of Jesus Compared with Others" (April 21, 1803), in *The Papers of Thomas Jefferson*, vol. 40: *4 March–10 July 1803*, ed. Barbara B. Oberg (Princeton, NJ: Princeton University Press, 2013), 253–255; *The Papers of Thomas Jefferson Digital Edition*, ed. James P. McClure and J. Jefferson Looney (Charlottesville: University of Virginia Press, Rotunda, 2008–2022), accessed July 30, 2022, https://rotunda-upress-virginia-edu.proxy.lib.duke.edu/founders/TSJN-01–40–02–0178–0001.

20   Curtis W. Freeman, "God in Three Persons: Baptist Unitarianism and the Trinity," *Perspectives in Religious Studies* 33, no. 3 (2006), 324; Freeman, *Contesting Catholicity: Theology for Other Baptists* (Waco, TX: Baylor University Press, 2014), 181.

21   H. Richard Niebuhr described three Unitarianisms in Christianity (i.e., of the Father, the Son, and the Spirit) in "The Doctrine of the Trinity and the Unity of the Church," *Theology Today* 3, no. 3 (1946): 371–84.

22   Malcolm B. Yarnell III, *God the Trinity: Biblical Portraits* (Nashville: Broadman and Holman, 2016), vii.

23   James B. Torrance, *Worship Community and the Triune God of Grace* (Downers Grove, IL: InterVarsity Press, 1996), 20.

24   Torrance, *Worship Community and the Triune God of Grace*, 21.

25   Augustine, "On the Trinity," 15.2.2, in *The Nicene and Post-Nicene Fathers*, 3:200.

26   William Blake, "Holy Trinity" pencil drawing, from the Notebook of William Blake, British Library, London.

27   Sarah Coakley, *God, Sexuality, and the Self: An Essay 'On the Trinity'* (Cambridge, UK: Cambridge University Press, 2013), 255–56.

28 *The Book of Common Prayer*, according to use in the Episcopal Church, 58.

MYSTERY 4 FOUR SENSES: READING LITERALLY
AND SPIRITUALLY

1 Bunyan, *The Pilgrim's Progress*, 187.
2 Thomas Aquinas, *Summa Theologiae*, I.10, trans. the Fathers of the English Dominican Province, in *The Collected Works of St. Thomas Aquinas*, Electronic Edition (Charlottesville, VA: InteLex Corp./Past Masters, 1993).
3 C. H. Spurgeon, *Lectures to My Students* (Grand Rapids, MI: Zondervan, 1962), 97.
4 E. S. James, "The Invincible Gospel," sermon preached at the 1941 Baptist General Convention of Texas (Vernon, TX: First Baptist Church, n.d.).
5 Krister Stendahl, "Biblical Theology, Contemporary," *Interpreter's Dictionary of the Bible*, ed. George Buttrick (Nashville: Abingdon, 1962), 1:418–32.
6 Richard B. Hays, *Reading Backwards: Figural Christology and the Fourfold Gospel Witness* (Waco, TX: Baylor University Press, 2016). Hays makes a similar argument about Paul's use of the Old Testament in his earlier work, *Echoes of Scripture in the Letters of Paul* (New Haven, CT: Yale University Press, 1989), 13. Hays describes Paul's interpretation of the Scripture as a creative and imaginative variation of Jewish Midrash that he calls dialectical intertextuality. *Echoes of Scripture in the Letters of Paul*, 176–77.
7 Jerome, "The Homilies of Saint Jerome," Homily 80 (VI), On Mark 9.1–7, trans. Marie Liguori Ewald, in *The Fathers of the Church* (Washington, DC: The Catholic University of America Press, 1966), 57:159.
8 Augustine, "On Christian Doctrine," Preface 6 and 1.39.43, trans. J. F. Shaw, in *The Nicene and Post-Nicene Fathers*, first series, ed. Philip Schaff (Grand Rapids, MI: Eerdmans, 1977), 2:520, 534.
9 Augustine, "On Christian Doctrine," 1.36.40, *The Nicene and Post-Nicene Fathers*, 2:533.

10 John Cassian, "The Conferences," 14.8.1–7, trans. Boniface Ramsey, in *Ancient Christian Testament Interpretation from Augustine to the Young Luther* (Cambridge, MA: Harvard University Press, 1969), 9–149.

11 Henri de Lubac, *Medieval Exegesis: The Four Senses of Scripture*, 2 vols., trans. Mark Sebanc (Grand Rapids, MI: Eerdmans, 1998–2000), 1:1; Henri Crouzel, "Spiritual Exegesis," in *Encyclopedia of Theology*, ed. Karl Rahner (New York: Seabury Press, 1975), 129–33.

12 Henri de Lubac, *Theological Fragments*, trans. Rebecca Howell Balinski (San Francisco: Ignatius, 1989), 114.

13 Augustine, "Questions on the Gospels," 2.19, trans. Roland J. Teske, in *The Works of Saint Augustine* (Hyde Park, NY: New City Press, 2014), 15/16:388–89.

14 C. H. Dodd, *The Parables of the Kingdom* (New York: Scribners, 1961), 2.

15 Dodd, *The Parables of the Kingdom*, 3–7.

16 Amy-Jill Levine, "The Many Faces of the Good Samaritan—Mostly Wrong," *Biblical Archaeology Review* 38, no. 1 (January/February 2012), 24, 68; Levine, "Go and Do Likewise: Lessons from the Parable of the Good Samaritan," *America: The Jesuit Review* 211, no. 8 (September 29, 2014): 16–18.

17 Origen, "Homilies on Luke," Homily 34, Luke 10:25–37, trans. Joseph T. Lienhard, in *The Fathers of the Church* (Washington, DC: The Catholic University of America Press, 1996), 94:137–41.

18 Henri de Lubac, *The Sources of Revelation*, trans. Luke O'Neill (New York: Herder and Herder, 1968), vii. See Lubac, *Medieval Exegesis*; and Jean Danielou, *From Shadows to Reality: Studies in Biblical Typology of the Fathers*, trans. Wulstan Hibberd (London: Burns and Oates, 1960).

19 Lubac, *The Sources of Revelation*, 12.

20 Lubac, *The Sources of Revelation*, 25–31.

21 Andrew Louth, *Discerning the Mystery: An Essay on the Nature of Theology* (Oxford: Clarendon Press, 1983), 111–13.

22 Raymond E. Brown, *The Sensus Plenior of Sacred Scripture* (Baltimore: St. Mary's Press, 1955; repr., Eugene, OR: Wipf and Stock, 2008), 88–92.

23 Curtis W. Freeman, "Toward a *Sensus Fidelium* for an Evangelical Church," in *The Nature of Confession: Evangelicals and Postliberal in Conversation*, ed. Timothy R. Phillips and Dennis L. Okholm (Downers Grove, IL: InterVarsity Press, 1996), 168–79.

24 Abraham Joshua Heschel, *God in Search of Man* (New York: Farrar, Strauss and Giroux, 1955), 252.

25 Arnoul of Boheriss, *Speculum monachorum*, 1, quoted in Jean Leclecq, *The Love of Learning and the Desire for God*, trans. Cathearine Misrahi (New York: Fordham University Press, 1982), 73.

26 Dietrich Bonhoeffer, *Psalms: The Prayer Book of the Bible*, trans. James H. Burtness (Minneapolis: Augsburg, 1970), 18–19.

27 Stephen B. Chapman, "Who Prays the Psalms? Bonhoeffer's Christological Concentration," *Toronto Journal of Theology* 37, no. 2 (Fall 2021): 168.

28 Robert L. Wilken, "The Lives of the Saints and the Pursuit of Virtue," *First Things* 1, no. 88 (December 1990): 45–51.

29 Karl Rahner, *The Theology of the Spiritual Life*, trans. Karl H. Kruger and Boniface Kruger, in *Theological Investigations* (Baltimore: Helicon, 1967), 3:100.

30 Alban Butler, *Butler's Lives of the Saints*, ed. Paul Burns, 12 vols. (Collegeville, MN: Liturgical Press, 1995–2000); Robert Ellsberg, *All Saints: Daily Reflections on Saints, Prophets, and Witnesses for Our Time* (New York: Crossroad, 2004).

31 Stephen E. Fowl and L. Gregory Jones, *Reading in Communion: Scripture and Ethics in Christian Life* (Grand Rapids, MI: Eerdmans, 1991), 56.

32 Paul S. Fiddes, "Dual Citizenship in Athens and Jerusalem: The Place of the Christian Scholar in the Life of the Church" (Founders Day Address for a conference on Christian Life and Witness: From the Academy to the Church, Georgetown College, Georgetown, KY, January 24, 2012). See Fiddes's chapter by the same title in Anthony R. Cross and Ruth M. B. Gouldbourne, eds., *Questions of Identity: Essays in Honour of Brian Haymes*, Centre for Baptist History and Heritage Studies 6 (Oxford: Regent's Park College, 2011), 137.

33 Edward Winslow, *Hypocrisie Unmasked: A True Relation of the Proceedings of the Governor and Company of Massachusetts against*

Samuel Gorton of Rhode Island (London: Rich. Cotes, 1646; repr. New York: Burt Franklin, 1968), 97; William Bradford, *Bradford's History 'Of Plimouth Plantation' from the Original Manuscript with a Report of the Proceedings Incident to the Return of the Manuscript to Massachusetts* (Boston: Wright and Potter, 1899), 71–83. See also Walter H. Burgess, *John Robinson, Pastor of the Pilgrim Fathers: A Study of His Life and Times* (New York: Harcourt, Brace and Howe, 1920), 239–40; Robert Ashton, ed., *The Works of John Robinson: Pastor of the Pilgrim Fathers* (London: John Snow, 1851), 1:xliv–xlv.

34 Mikael Broadway, et al., "Re-Envisioning Baptist Identity: A Manifesto for Baptist Communities in North America," *Baptists Today,* June 26, 1997, 8; also Curtis W. Freeman, "Can Baptist Theology Be Revisioned?" *Perspectives in Religious Studies* 24, no. 3 (1997): 304–5.

35 Ernest Payne, *The Fellowship of Believers: Baptist Thought and Practice, Yesterday and Today*, 2nd ed. (London: Carey Kingsgate, 1952), 18.

36 Northrop Frye, "William Blake," in *The English Romantic Poets and Essayists*, ed. Lawrence Houtchens and and Carolyn Washburn Houtchens (New York: Modern Language Association, 1957), 18.

37 Northrop Frye, *Northrop Frye in Conversation*, ed. David Cayley (Concord, ON: Anansi, 1992), 48; cited by Ian Singer, Introduction to *Fearful Symmetry*, ed. Nicholas Halmi, in *The Collected Works of Northrop Frye*, vol. 14 (Toronto: University of Toronto Press, 1996), xxxii. Frye's line was about the comparison between Milton and Blake.

38 Bunyan, "The Author's Apology," in *The Pilgrim's Progress*, 4.

39 William Blake, *A Vision of Last Judgment*, in *Blake Complete Writings*, ed. Geoffrey Keynes (London: Oxford University Press, 1969), 604.

40 Blake, "Annotations to Berkeley's 'Siris,'" in *Blake Complete Writings*, 774; Harold Bloom, *The Complete Poetry and Prose of William Blake*, ed. David V. Erdman (Berkeley: University of California Press, 2008), 934–35.

41 William Blake, "Mercy and Truth Are Met Together, Righteousness and Peace Have Kissed Each Other," 1803, in the Victoria and Albert Museum, London.

42 Bunyan, *Grace Abounding to the Chief of Sinners*, §136; 36.
43 Bunyan, *Grace Abounding*, §226; 58. Typology is a form of spiritual interpretation, very much like allegory, in which an Old Testament event, institution, or person (the *type*) prefigures a New Testament event, institution, or person (the *antitype*). Typology is often, though not exclusively, Christological. The focus of typology tends to be narrower than allegory, but the two are closely related. It would be a misunderstanding to describe allegory as opposed to typology.
44 Bunyan, *Grace Abounding*, §230 and §239; 59–61.

MYSTERY 5 FIVE ACTS: THE SCOPE OF GOD'S STORY

1 Bunyan, *The Pilgrim's Progress*, 212.
2 Ellen F. Davis and Richard B. Hays, eds. *The Art of Reading Scripture* (Grand Rapids, MI: Eerdmans, 2003), 1–5.
3 Jenson, *Systematic Theology, Volume 1: The Triune God* (New York: Oxford, 1997), 63.
4 Aristotle, *Poetics*, 7.26–33, 1450b–1451a, trans. Ingram Bywater, in *The Basic Works of Aristotle*, ed. Richard McKeon (New York: Random House, 1941), 1462.
5 Frank Kermode, *The Sense of an Ending: Studies in the Theory of Fiction* (New York: Oxford, 1966), 3–31.
6 Norman Cohn, *The Pursuit of the Millennium: Revolutionary Millenarians and Mystical Anarchists of the Middle Ages*, rev. ed. (New York: Oxford, 1970).
7 J. R. R. Tolkien, "On Fairy-Stories," in *Tree and Leaf* (London: Unwin Books, 1964), 60–63.
8 Joel Marcus, *Mark 1–8*, in *The Anchor Bible* (New York: Doubleday, 2000), 342.
9 Hans W. Frei, *The Identity of Jesus Christ: The Hermeneutical Bases of Dogmatic Theology* (Eugene, OR: Wipf and Stock, 1997).
10 Hans W. Frei, *The Eclipse of Biblical Narrative: A Study in Eighteenth and Nineteenth Century Hermeneutics* (New Haven, CT: Yale University Press, 1974), 124–54; George A. Lindbeck, "The Bible as Realistic Narrative," *Journal of Ecumenical Studies* 17, no. 1 (1980): 81–85.

11 Eric Auerbach, *Mimesis: The Representation of Reality in Western Literature*, trans. Willard R. Trask (Princeton, NJ: Princeton University Press, 1953), 14–15.

12 Rudolf Otto, *The Idea of the Holy*, 2nd ed., trans. John W. Harvey (London: Oxford, 1958), 12–24.

13 Ellen F. Davis, *Opening Israel's Scriptures* (New York: Oxford, 2019), 55, 62–71.

14 Although I arrived at the five-act structure independently, my framework is similar to and sympathetic with the account of Samuel Wells, *Improvisation: The Drama of Christian Ethics* (Grand Rapids, MI: Brazos Press, 2004), 52–57. I have also learned from N. T. Wright, who describes Scripture as a five-act play: creation, fall, Israel, Jesus, and the church. Wright suggests that we are currently living in the fifth act, the time of the church, which began with Easter and Pentecost. Wright, "How Can the Bible Be Authoritative?" *Vox Evangelica* 21 (1991): 7–32, esp. 18–19; Wright, *Scripture and the Authority of God* (New York: Harper One, 2005), 122–23; Wright, *The New Testament and the People of God* (Minneapolis: Fortress, 1992), 141–42. Others who have been helpful to me in this understanding of the narrative scope of Scripture are Kevin J. Vanhoozer, *Four Views on Moving beyond the Bible to Theology*, ed. Gary T. Meadors (Grand Rapids, MI: Zondervan, 2009); Vanhoozer, *The Drama of Doctrine: A Canonical-Linguistic Approach to Christian Theology* (Louisville, KY: Westminster/John Knox, 2005), 2–3; Joshua Strahan, *The Basics of Christian Belief: Bible, Theology, and Life's Big Questions* (Grand Rapids, MI: Baker, 2020), 15–69; and Gabriel Fackre, *The Christian Story: A Narrative Interpretation of Christian Doctrine*, rev. ed. (Grand Rapids, MI: Eerdmans, 1984). I have also learned from the earlier Christian practice displayed by Irenaeus, *The Proof of the Apostolic Preaching*, which is a catechetical teaching aid used in the early church to tell the story of salvation. Irenaeus, *The Proof of the Apostolic Preaching*, trans. Armitage Robinson (New York: Macmillan, 1920); Everett Ferguson, "Irenaeus' *Proof of the Apostolic Preaching* and Early Catechetical Instruction," in *The Early Church at Work and Worship*, vol. 2 *Catechesis, Baptism, Eschatology, and Martyrdom* (Eugene, OR: Cascade, 2014), 1–17.

15 Paul M. Blowers, *Drama of the Divine Economy: Creator and Creation in Early Christian Theology and Piety* (Oxford: Oxford University Press, 2012), 15.

16 J. L. Austin, *How to Do Things with Words*, 2nd ed., ed. J. O. Urmson and Marina Sbisà (Cambridge, MA: Harvard University Press, 1975), 1–7.

17 Dante Alighieri, *The Divine Comedy*, trans. John Ciardi, *Paradiso*, 33:146 (New York: W. W. Norton, 1970), 601.

18 McClendon, *Doctrine*, 285.

19 Hans Conzelmann, *Die Mitte der Zeit: Studien zur Theologie des Lukas* (Tübingen: Mohr, 1954); *The Theology of St. Luke,* trans. Geoffrey Buswell (Philadelphia: Fortress, 1982).

20 "Didache," 10.6, trans. James A. Kleist, in *Ancient Christian Writers* (New York: Newman Press, 1948), 6:21.

21 Wells, *Improvisation*, 55.

22 Nicholas Lash, *Theology on the Way to Emmaus* (London: SCM Press, 1986), 41.

23 William Blake, "The Lord Answering Job Out of the Whirlwind," 1805. The Butts set. The Morgan Library and Museum, New York.

24 Karl Barth, *Church Dogmatics*, IV/3.1, trans. G. W. Bromiley (Edinburgh: T. & T. Clark, 1961), 407–8.

MYSTERY 6 SIX SEASONS: THE CHURCH YEAR

1 Bunyan, *The Pilgrim's Progress*, 195. Psalm 23 from Thomas Sternhold and John Hopkins, *The Whole Book of Psalms Collected into English Metre* (London: John Daye, 1584), 76–77.

2 Daniel Defoe, *Robinson Crusoe*, ed. Michael Shinagel (New York: W. W. North & Company, 1994), 48.

3 Augustine, *Confessions*, 11.14.17, trans. John K. Ryan (New York: Doubleday/Image,1960), 287.

4 Augustine, *Confessions*, 11.20.26, 292–93.

5 Augustine, *Confessions*, 11.30.40–11.31.41, 302–4.

6 Augustine, *Confessions*, 1.1.1, 43.

7 Abraham Joshua Heschel, *Sabbath: Its Meaning for Modern Man* (New York: Farrar, Straus and Giroux, 2005), 8.

8   Ignatius, "Letter to the Magnesians," 9, in *Early Christian Fathers*, 96. For a wide range of Christian witnesses to worship on Sunday, see Everett Ferguson, *Early Christians Speak: Faith and Life in the First Three Centuries* (Austin, TX: Sweet Publishing, 1971), 67–79.

9   Jürgen Moltmann, *God in Creation: A New Theology of Creation and the Spirit of God* (Minneapolis: Fortress, 1993), 294.

10 Norman Wirzba, *Living the Sabbath: Discovering the Rhythms of Rest and Delight* (Grand Rapids, MI: Brazos Press, 2006), 43.

11 Lash, *Easter in Ordinary*, 286–96.

12 Melitio of Sardis, *On Pascha*, 2–3, trans. Alistair Stewart-Sykes (Yonkers, NY: St. Vladimir's Seminary Press, 2001), 50–51.

13 Melitio of Sardis, *On Pascha*, 46, 63–64, 66, and 69–70.

14 The Heidelberg Catechism, §37, in Presbyterian Church (USA), *Book of Confessions*, rev. study ed. (Louisville, KY: Westminster/John Knox Press, 2017), 80.

15 Adolf Adam, *The Liturgical Year: Its History and Its Meaning after the Reform of the Liturgy*, trans. Matthew J. O'Connell (New York: Pueblo Publishing, 1981), 21–23.

16 Thomas J. Talley, *The Origins of the Liturgical Year* (New York: Pueblo Publishing, 1986), 1–77; Eusebius, "Church History," 5.24, trans. Arthur Cushman McGiffert, in *The Nicene and Post-Nicene Fathers*, second series (Grand Rapids, MI: Eerdmans, 1976), 1:242–44; Sozomenus, "Church History," 7.18–19, trans. Chester D. Hartranft, in *The Nicene and Post-Nicene Fathers*, second series (Grand Rapids, MI: Eerdmans, 1973), 2:388–92; "The Seven Ecumenical Councils," trans. Henry R. Percival, in *The Nicene and Post-Nicene Fathers*, second series (Grand Rapids, MI: Eerdmans, 1977), 14:54–56.

17 The conference was the 1987 Pastors School at Stetson University in Deland, Florida. The preacher was William H. Willimon, minister to the university and professor of Christian Ministry at Duke University Divinity School. His lectures were on Luke–Acts. The comments about the Christian year are my recollection.

18 John Smyth, *The Differences of the Churches of the Separation*, 10.7, in *The Works of John Smyth*, ed. W. T. Whitley (Cambridge,

UK: Cambridge University Press, 1915), 1:4. For an account of the Free Church resistance to formal worship, see Christopher J. Ellis, *Gathering: A Theology and Spirituality of Worship in Free Church Tradition* (London: SCM Press, 2004), 37–99.

19 John Bunyan, "I Will Pray With the Spirit and With the Understanding Also," in *The Works of John Bunyan*, ed. George Offor, 3 vols. (Glasgow: W. G. Blackie and Son, 1854; repr., Carlisle, PA: Banner of Trust, 1991), 1:623.

20 John Calvin, *Institutes of the Christian Religion*, 2.16.5, ed. John T. McNeill and trans. Ford Lewis Battles (Philadelphia: Westminster Press, 1960), 1:507.

21 Robert E. Webber, *Ancient-Future Time: Forming Spirituality through the Christian Year* (Grand Rapids, MI: Baker, 2004), 31; Hoyt L. Hickman et al., *The New Handbook of the Christian Year* (Nashville: Abingdon, 1992), 51–257.

22 The Nicene Creed, trans. English Language Liturgical Consultation (ELLC) in *Praying Together* (Nashville: Abingdon, 1988), 17.

23 Athanasius, *On the Incarnation of the Word*, §9 (Crestwood, NY: St Vladimir's Seminary Press, 1944), 35.

24 John Milton, *On the Morning of Christ's Nativity*, XI (Cambridge, UK: Cambridge University Press, 1923), 18. Blake's illustration follows the hymn on page 19.

25 Bunyan, *The Pilgrim's Progress*, 195.

MYSTERY 7 SEVEN SACRAMENTAL SIGNS: HOLY THINGS FOR HOLY PEOPLE

1 Bunyan, *The Pilgrim's Progress*, 193.
2 Virginia Cary Hudson, *O Ye Jigs & Juleps!* (New York: Macmillan, 1962), 1.
3 Gordon W. Lathrop, *Holy Things: A Liturgical Theology* (Minneapolis: Fortress Press, 1993), 116.
4 "Constitutions of the Holy Apostles," VIII.13, trans. James Donaldson, in *The Ante-Nicene Fathers*, ed. Alexander Roberts, James Donaldson, and A. Cleveland Coxe (Grand Rapids, MI: Eerdmans,1979), 7:490.

5 "Constitutions of the Holy Apostles," VIII.7, *The Ante-Nicene Fathers*, 7:484; "Didache," 9.5, in *Ancient Christian Writers*, 6:20.

6 Martin Luther, "The Babylonian Captivity of the Church," trans. A. T. W. Steinhäuser and rev. Frederick C. Ahrens and Abdel Ross Wentz in *Luther's Works* (Philadelphia: Fortress, 1959), 36:112–13.

7 Martin Luther, "The Estate of Marriage," trans. Walther I. Brandt in *Luther's Works* (Philadelphia: Fortress Press, 1962), 45:40.

8 Michel de Certeau, *The Practice of Everyday Life*, trans. Steven F. Rendall (Berkeley: University of California Press, 1984), xvii–xix.

9 Kathleen Norris, *Quotidian Mysteries: Laundry, Liturgy, and "Women's Work"* (Mahwah, NJ: Paulist Press, 1998), 3.

10 *The Book of Common Prayer*, "An Outline of the Faith," 857.

11 Augustine, "Letter to Marcelinus," 138.7, trans. J. G. Cunningham, *The Nicene and Post-Nicene Fathers* (Grand Rapids, MI: Eerdmans, 1979), 1:483.

12 Augustine of Hippo, "Sermon 272," *Ad Infantes, de Sacramento, in Patrologia Cursus Completus, Series Latina*, ed. J. P. Migne (Paris: Migne, 1865), 38:1246–48.

13 *The Westminster Shorter Catechism*, §92, in *Book of Confessions*, 277.

14 Herbert McCabe, *God Matters* (London: Geoffrey Chapman, 1987), 169.

15 McClendon, *Doctrine*, 381–82.

16 Peter Lombard, *The Sentences*, trans. Giulio Silano, *Book 4: On the Doctrine of Signs*, IV.1.4.2 (Toronto: Pontifical Institute of Mediaeval Studies, 2010), 4.

17 John Calvin, *The Institutes of the Christian Religion*, IV.14.3, ed. John T. McNeill and trans. Ford Lewis Battles (Philadelphia: Westminster, 1960), 1278.

18 John E. Colwell, *Promise and Presence: An Exploration of Sacramental Theology* (Milton Keynes: Paternoster, 2005), 11.

19 Hercules Collins, *An Orthodox Catechism* (London: n.p., 1680), 25.

20 William Kiffin, *A Sober Discourse of Right to Church Communion* (London: George Larkin, 1681), 25.

21 Kiffin, *A Sober Discourse of Right to Church Communion*, 42–43.

22 "The Orthodox Creed," 19, in *Baptist Confessions of Faith*, 311–12.

23 Michael A. G. Haykin, *Amidst Us Our Belovèd Stands: Recovering Sacrament in the Baptist Tradition* (Bellingham, WA: Lexham Press, 2022), 120–21.

24 Friedrich von Hügel, "The Convictions Common to Catholicism and Protestantism," in *Essays and Addresses on the Philosophy of Religion* (London: J. M. Dent; New York: E. P. Dutton, 1924), 251.

25 *The Westminster Shorter Catechism*, §92 (Richmond, VA: Presbyterian Committee of Publication, n.d.).

26 Bernard Cooke, *Sacraments and Sacramentality* (Mystic, CT: Twenty-Third Publications, 1983), 63–66.

27 Donald M. Baillie, *The Theology of the Sacraments* (New York: Scribner's Sons, 1957), 66–67.

28 Martin Luther, "On the Councils and the Church," trans. Charles M. Jacobs, rev. Eric W. Gritsch, in *Luther's Works* (Philadelphia: Fortress, 1966), 41:148–66.

29 Dietrich Philips, "The Church of God," in *Spiritual and Anabaptist Writers*, ed. George H. Williams (Philadelphia: Westminster Press, 1957), 240–55.

30 David Benedict, *A General History of the Baptist Denomination in America and Other Parts of the World* (New York: Lewis Colby and Co., 1848), 686.

31 Dorothy C. Bass, *Practicing Our Faith* (San Francisco: Josey-Bass Publishers, 1997), xi, 2; Alasdair MacIntyre, *After Virtue* (Notre Dame, IN: University of Notre Dame Press, 1981), 175.

32 John L. Austin, *How to Do Things with Words*, 2nd ed. (Oxford: Oxford University Press, 1975), Lecture VIII, 94–108; John R. Searle, *Speech Acts* (London: Cambridge University Press, 1969), 22–26.

33 David C. Steinmetz, "Luther and the Ascent of Jacob's Ladder," *Church History* 55, no. 2 (Jun. 1986): 179–192; Martin Luther, "Lectures on Genesis," in *Luther's Works* (St. Louis: Concordia Publishing House, 1968), 5:201–65; Luther, "On the Councils and the Church," in *Luther's Works* (Philadelphia, PA: Fortress, 1966), 41:150.

34 John Calvin, *Commentary on Genesis*, 2 vols., trans. John King (Grand Rapids, MI: Eerdmans, 1948), 2:113.

35 Calvin, *The Institutes of the Christian Religion*, IV.17.31, 1403.

36 Bunyan, *The Pilgrim's Progress*, 193.

37 William Blake (1757–1827), Jacob's Ladder, or Jacob's Dream (1799–1806), pen and gray ink and watercolor on paper, 39.8 × 30.6 cm, The British Museum, London. Courtesy of and © Trustees of the British Museum.

Conclusion: Things Deep, Hid, and Mysterious

1 Bunyan, *The Pilgrim's Progress*, 100.

2 William Blake, *The Pilgrims Meet the Shepherds of the Delectable Mountains*, an illustration to Bunyan's *Pilgrim's Progress*. Watercolor by Blake and another hand, probably Mrs. Blake, 13 × 18.7 cm., datable to c. 1824–27.

3 Bunyan, *The Pilgrim's Progress*, 97–100.

4 Bunyan, *The Pilgrim's Progress*, 129.

5 Bunyan, *The Pilgrim's Progress*, 129.

6 William Williams, "Guide Me O Thou Great Jehovah," #39, trans. Peter Williams, in *A Select Collection of Hymns*, 5th ed., ed. Selina Hastings, Countess of Huntingdon (London: Hughes and Walsh, 1780), 59–60.

7 Bunyan, *The Pilgrim's Progress*, 257–61.

8 Samuel Stennett, "The Promised Land," in *A Selection of Hymns*, ed. John Rippon (London: Thomas Wilkins, 1787), 584.

9 Alexander Schmemann, *For the Life of the World: Sacraments and Orthodoxy* (Crestwood, NY: St. Vladimir's Seminary Press, 2004), 99–100.

10 The Apostles' Creed, trans. English Language Liturgical Consultation (ELLC) in *Praying Together* (Nashville: Abingdon, 1988), 22.

11 The Apostles' Creed, in *Praying Together*, 23.

12 Wayne Grudem, *Systematic Theology: An Introduction to Biblical Doctrine* (Grand Rapids, MI: Zondervan, 1994), 585–94; Grudem, "He Did Not Descend into Hell: A Plea for Following Scripture Instead of the Apostles' Creed," *Journal of the*

Evangelical Theological Society 34, no. 1 (March 1991): 103–13. See also J. N. D. Kelly, *Early Christian Creeds*, 3rd ed. (New York: Longman, 1972), 378; and Philip Schaff, *The Creeds of Christendom*, 3 vols., 6th ed. (New York: Harper, 1931), 1:21, fn 36.

13 Dante Alighieri, *The Divine Comedy*, trans. John Ciardi, *Inferno*, 4.52–63 (New York: W. W. Norton, 1970), 20–21; William Langland, *Piers Plowman* (The C Version), XX, trans. George Economou (Philadelphia: University of Pennsylvania Press, 1996), 182–95. For the earliest apocryphal references to the harrowing of hell, see *The Gospel of Nicodemus*, 4(20)–10(26), in *The Apocryphal Jesus: Legends of the Early Church*, ed. J. K. Elliott (New York: Oxford University Press, 1996), 99–102. For Protestant appropriations, see Martin Luther, "Torgau Sermon on Christ's Descent into Hell and Resurrection," 1532, in *Sources and Contexts of The Book of Concord*, edited by Robert Kolb and James A. Nestingen (Minneapolis: Fortress Press, 2001), 246–50; and C. S. Lewis, *The Lion, the Witch, and the Wardrobe* (New York: Macmillan, 1988), 142–44.

14 Jürgen Moltmann, *The Crucified God: The Cross of Christ as the Foundation and Criticism of Christian Theology*, trans. R. A. Wilson and John Bowden (New York: Harper, 1974), 151–52; Hans Urs von Balthasar, *Mysterium Paschale: The Mystery of Easter*, trans. Aidan Nichols (San Francisco: Ignatius Press, 1990), 148–87.

15 Matthew Y. Emerson, *He Descended into the Dead: An Evangelical Theology of Holy Saturday* (Downers Grove, IL: InterVarsity, 2019), 219–21.

16 Alighieri, *The Divine Comedy*, 3.9; Ciardi, *Inferno*, 13.

17 Karl Barth, *Deliverance to the Captives*, trans. Marguerite Wieser (New York: Harper & Row, 1961); Barth, *Call for God*, trans. A. T. Mackay (New York: Harper & Row, 1967).

18 Martin Schwartz, "Preaching in the Basel Prison," in *Karl Barth in der Strafanstalt*, trans. Joseph Longarino. Center for Barth Studies, Princeton Theological Seminary, accessed July 9, 2022, https://barth.ptsem.edu/preaching-in-the-basel-prison/.

19 Barth, *Deliverance to the Captives*, 86.

20 Barth, *Deliverance to the Captives*, 88.

21 Barth, *Deliverance to the Captives*, 144–51.

22 Martin Luther, *The Pious and Learned Commentary of Martin Luther on the First Twenty-Two Psalms*, vol. 4, in *Select Works of Martin Luther*, trans. Henry Cole (London: T. Bensley, 1826), 360–61. Luther's commentary of Psalm 22 is sadly omitted from the American edition of *Luther's Works*, but the original may be found in D. Martin Luther's *Werke: Kritische Gesamtausgabe* (Weimar: Hermann Böhlau, 1892), 5:603–4.

23 John Calvin, "Psychopannychia," in *Tracts and Treatises in Defense of the Reformed Faith*, trans. Henry Beveridge, 3 vols. (Grand Rapids, MI: Eerdmans, 1958), 3:480.

24 Calvin, *The Institutes of the Christian Religion*, 2.16.10, 1:516.

25 Calvin, *Institutes of the Christian Religion*, 2.16.12, 1:520.

26 Calvin, "Psychopannychia," in *Tracts and Treatises*, 3:483.

27 *The Heidelberg Catechism*, §44, in *Book of Confessions*, 81.

28 Preston Hill, "When Jesus Doubted God: Perspectives from Calvin on Post-Traumatic Faith," *The Other Journal*, February 10, 2022, accessed July 12, 2022, https://theotherjournal.com/2022/02/10/doubt-calvin-post-traumatic-faith/.

29 Dewey Williams, *Finding Joy on Death Row: Unexpected Lessons from Lives We Discarded* (Nashville: Dexterity Press, 2023).

30 Stephen H. Webb, "Why von Balthasar Was Wrong about Holy Saturday," *First Things*, August 27, 2013, web exclusive, accessed July 9, 2022, https://www.firstthings.com/web-exclusives/2013/08/why-von-balthasar-was-wrong-about-holy-saturday.

31 Thomas A. Dorsey, *Take My Hand Precious Lord* (Chicago: Hill and Range Songs, 1938).

Bibliography

Adam, Adolf. *The Liturgical Year: Its History and Its Meaning after the Reform of the Liturgy*. Translated by Matthew J. O'Connell. New York: Pueblo Publishing, 1981.

Alighieri, Dante. *The Divine Comedy*. Translated by John Ciardi. New York: W. W. Norton, 1970.

Anselm. *The Prayers and Meditations of Saint Anselm*. Translated by Benedicta Ward. New York: Penguin, 1973.

Aquinas, Thomas. *Summa Theologiae*. Translated by the Fathers of the English Dominican Province. In *The Collected Works of St. Thomas Aquinas*, Electronic Edition. Charlottesville, VA: InteLex Corp/Past Masters, 1993.

Aristotle. *The Basic Works of Aristotle*. Edited by Richard McKeon. New York: Random House, 1941.

Athanasius. "Against the Arians." Translated by John Henry Newman and Archibald Robertson. In *The Nicene and Post-Nicene Fathers*, Second Series, edited by Philip Schaff and Henry Wace, 303–447. Vol. 4. Grand Rapids, MI: Eerdmans, 1978.

———. *On the Incarnation of the Word*. Crestwood, NY: St. Vladimir's Seminary Press, 1944.

Auerbach, Eric. *Mimesis: The Representation of Reality in Western Literature*. Translated by Willard R. Trask. Princeton, NJ: Princeton University Press, 1953.

Augustine. *City of God*. Translated by Henry Bettenson. New York: Penguin, 1984.

———. *Confessions*. Translated by John K. Ryan. New York: Doubleday/Image, 1960.

———. "Letters." Translated by J. G. Cunningham. In *The Nicene and Post-Nicene Fathers*, edited by Philip Schaff, 209–593. Vol. 1. Grand Rapids, MI: Eerdmans, 1979.

———. "On Christian Doctrine." Translated by J. F. Shaw. In *The Nicene and Post-Nicene Fathers*, First Series, edited by Philip Schaff, 512–97. Vol. 2. Grand Rapids, MI: Eerdmans, 1977.

———. "On Rebuke and Grace." Translated by Peter Holmes and Robert Ernest Wallis, and revised by Benjamin B. Warfield. In *The Nicene and Post Nicene Fathers*, edited by Philip Schaff, 471–91. Vol. 5. Grand Rapids, MI: Eerdmans, 1971.

———. "On the Spirit and the Letter." Translated by Benjamin B. Warfield. In *The Nicene and Post Nicene Fathers*, edited by Philip Schaff, 83–113. Vol. 5. Grand Rapids, MI: Eerdmans, 1978.

———. "On the Trinity." Translated by Arthur West Haddan and William G. T. Shedd. In *The Nicene and Post-Nicene Fathers*, edited by Philip Schaff, 1–228. Vol. 3. Grand Rapids, MI: Eerdmans, 1978.

———. "Questions on the Gospels." Translated by Roland J. Teske. In *The Works of Saint Augustine*, edited by Boniface Ramsey, 349–415. Vols. 15–16. Hyde Park, NY: New City Press, 2014.

———. "Sermon 272." In *Ad Infantes, de Sacramento. Patrologia Latina*, edited by J. P. Migne, 1246–48. Vol. 38. Paris: Migne, 1865.

Austin, J. L. *How to Do Things with Words*. 2nd ed. Edited by J. O. Urmson and Marina Sbisà. Cambridge, MA: Harvard University Press, 1975.

Baillie, D. M. *God Was in Christ: An Essay on Incarnation and Atonement*. New York: Scribners, 1948.

———. *The Theology of the Sacraments*. New York: Scribner's Sons, 1957.

Balthasar, Hans Urs von. *Mysterium Paschale: The Mystery of Easter*. Translated by Aidan Nichols. San Francisco: Ignatius Press, 1990.

Barnett, Victoria J. "German Protestantism and the Challenges of National Socialism." *American Baptist Quarterly* 37, no. 4 (2014): 388–404.

Barron, Robert. *The Priority of Christ: Toward a Postliberal Catholicism*. Grand Rapids, MI: Brazos Press, 2007.

Barth, Karl. *Call for God*. Translated by A. T. Mackay. New York: Harper & Row, 1967.

———. *Church Dogmatics*, I/1. Translated by G. W. Bromiley. Edinburgh: T & T Clark, 1957.

———. *Church Dogmatics*, I/2. Translated by G. T. Thomson and Harold Knight. Edinburgh: T & T Clark, 1956.

———. *Church Dogmatics*, II/1. Translated by T. H. L. Parker, W. B. Johnston, Harold Knight, and J. L. M. Haire. Edinburgh: T & T Clark, 1957.

———. *Church Dogmatics*, IV/1. Translated by G. W. Bromiley. Edinburgh: T & T Clark, 1956.

———. *Church Dogmatics*, IV/2. Translated by G. W. Bromiley and T. F. Torrance. Edinburgh: T & T Clark, 1958.

———. *Church Dogmatics*, IV/3.1. Translated by G. W. Bromiley. Edinburgh: T & T Clark, 1961.

———. *Deliverance to the Captives*. Translated by Marguerite Wieser. New York: Harper & Row, 1961.

Bass, Dorothy C. *Practicing Our Faith*. San Francisco: Josey-Bass Publishers, 1997.

Benedict, David. *A General History of the Baptist Denomination in America and Other Parts of the World*. New York: Lewis Colby, 1848.

Blake, William. *Blake Complete Writings*. Edited by Geoffrey Keynes. London: Oxford University Press, 1969.

———. *The Poetry and Prose of William Blake*. Edited by David V. Erdman. New York: Doubleday, 1970.

———. *William Blake The Complete Illuminated Books*. New York: Thames & Hudson, 2001.

Blowers, Paul M. *Drama of the Divine Economy: Creator and Creation in Early Christian Theology and Piety*. Oxford: Oxford University Press, 2012.

Bonhoeffer, Dietrich. *Psalms: The Prayer Book of the Bible*. Translated by James H. Burtness. Minneapolis: Augsburg, 1970.

Bradford, William. *History 'Of Plimouth Plantation.'* Boston, MA: Wright and Potter, 1899.

Broadway, Mikael, Curtis Freeman, Barry Harvey, James Wm. McClendon Jr., Elizabeth Newman, and Philip Thompson. "Re-Envisioning Baptist Identity: A Manifesto for Baptist Communities in North America." *Baptists Today*, June 26, 1997.

Brown, Raymond E. *The Sensus Plenior of Sacred Scripture*. Baltimore: St. Mary's Press, 1955. Reprint, Eugene, OR: Wipf & Stock, 2008.

Brumley, Jeff. "Ryan Burge Sifts the Data to Paint an Evolving Portrait of the 'Nones.'" *Baptist News Global*, April 1, 2021. Accessed July 31, 2022. https://baptistnews.com/article/ryan-burge-sifts-the-data-to-paint-an-evolving-portrait-of-the-nones/#.YubGNYTMKUk.

Bruce, F. F. *The Books and the Parchments*. Rev. ed. Old Tappan, NJ: Fleming H. Revell, 1963.

Buckley, Michael J. *At the Origins of Modern Atheism*. New Haven, CT: Yale University Press, 1990.

Buber, Martin. *I and Thou*. Translated by Walter Kaufmann. New York: Touchstone, 1970.

Bunyan, John. *Grace Abounding to the Chief of Sinners*. Edited by W. R. Owens. New York: Penguin, 1987.

———. *The Pilgrim's Progress*. Edited by N. H. Keeble. New York: Oxford, 1984.

———. *The Works of John Bunyan*. Edited by George Offor. 3 vols. Glasgow: W. G. Blackie and Son, 1854. Reprint, Carlisle, PA: Banner of Trust, 1991.

Burge, Ryan. *The Nones: Where They Came From, Who They Are, and Where They Are Going*. Minneapolis: Fortress, 2021.

Burgess, Walter H. *John Robinson, Pastor of the Pilgrim Fathers: A Study of His Life and Times*. New York: Harcourt, Brace & Howe, 1920.

Burrell, David B. *Aquinas: God and Action*. 3rd ed. Edited by Mary Budde Ragan. Eugene, OR: Wipf and Stock, 2016.

———. *Friendship and Ways to Truth*. Notre Dame, IN: University of Notre Dame Press, 2000.

Butler, Alban. *Butler's Lives of the Saints*. Edited by Paul Burns. 12 vols. Collegeville, MN: Liturgical Press, 1995–2000.

Buttrick, George, ed. *Interpreter's Dictionary of the Bible*. Nashville: Abingdon, 1962.

Calvin, John. *Commentary on Genesis*. 2 vols. Translated by John King. Grand Rapids, MI: Eerdmans, 1948.

———. *Institutes of the Christian Religion*. 2 vols. Edited by John T. McNeill. Translated by Ford Lewis Battles. Philadelphia: Westminster Press, 1960.

———. *Tracts and Treatises in Defense of the Reformed Faith*. 3 vols. Translated by Henry Beveridge. Grand Rapids, MI: Eerdmans, 1958.

Cassian, John. "The Conferences." Translated by Boniface Ramsey. In *Ancient Christian Writers*. Vol. 57. New York: Paulist Press, 1997.

Catholic Church. *Rite of Christian Initiation of Adults*. Study ed. Chicago: Liturgy Training, 1988.

Certeau, Michel de. *The Practice of Everyday Life*. Translated by Steven F. Rendall. Berkeley: University of California Press, 1984.

Chapman, Stephen B. "What Are We Reading? Canonicity and the Old Testament." *Word and World* 29, no. 4 (2009): 334–47.

———. "Who Prays the Psalms? Bonhoeffer's Christological Concentration." *Toronto Journal of Theology* 37, no. 2 (2021): 168–77.

Childs, Brevard S. *Biblical Theology of the Old and New Testaments*. Minneapolis: Fortress, 1992.

Clément, Oliver. *The Roots of Christian Mysticism*. 2nd ed. Hyde Park, NY: New City Press, 2019.

Coakley, Sarah. *God, Sexuality, and the Self: An Essay 'On the Trinity.'* Cambridge, UK: Cambridge University Press, 2013.

———. *Powers and Submissions: Spirituality, Philosophy, and Gender*. Oxford: Blackwell, 2002.

Cochrane, Arthur C. *The Church's Confessions under Hitler*. Philadelphia: Westminster Press, 1962.

Cohn, Norman. *The Pursuit of the Millennium: Revolutionary Millenarians and Mystical Anarchists of the Middle Ages*. Rev. ed. New York: Oxford, 1970.

Collins, Hercules. *An Orthodox Catechism*. London: n.p., 1680.

Colwell, John E. *Promise and Presence: An Exploration of Sacramental Theology*. Milton Keynes: Paternoster, 2005.

Congar, Yves. *Divided Christendom*. London: G. Bles, 1939.

Conklin, Jeff. "Wicked Problems and Social Complexity." In *Dialogue Mapping: Building Shared Understanding of Wicked Problems*. Chichester: Wiley, 2006.

"Constitutions of the Holy Apostles." Translated by James Donaldson. In *The Ante-Nicene Fathers*, edited by Alexander Roberts, James Donaldson, and A. Cleveland Coxe, 391–505. Vol. 7. Grand Rapids, MI: Eerdmans, 1979.

Conzelmann, Hans. *The Theology of St. Luke*. Translated by Geoffrey Buswell. Philadelphia: Fortress, 1982.

Cooke, Bernard. *Sacraments and Sacramentality*. Mystic, CT: Twenty-Third Publications, 1983.

Cowper, William, and John Newton. *Olney Hymns,* in Three Parts. London: T. Nelson and Sons, 1855.

Crouzel, Henri. "Spiritual Exegesis." In *Encyclopedia of Theology*, edited by Karl Rahner. New York: Seabury Press, 1975.

Cyril of Jerusalem. "Catechetical Lectures." Translated by Edwin Hamilton Gifford. In *The Nicene and Post-Nicene Fathers*, Second Series, edited by Philip Schaff and Henry Wace. Vol. 7. Grand Rapids, MI: Eerdmans, 1978.

Danielou, Jean. *From Shadows to Reality: Studies in Biblical Typology of the Fathers*. Translated by Wulstan Hibberd. London: Burns and Oates, 1960.

Davis, Ellen F. *Opening Israel's Scriptures*. New York: Oxford, 2019.

Davis, Ellen F. and Richard B. Hays, eds. *The Art of Reading Scripture*. Grand Rapids, MI: Eerdmans, 2003.

Defoe, Daniel. *Robinson Crusoe*. Edited by Michael Shinagel. New York: W. W. North & Company, 1994.

"Didache, or The Teaching of the Twelve Apostles." Translated by James A. Kleist. In *Ancient Christian Writers*, 1–25. Vol. 6. New York: Newman Press, 1948.

Dodd, C. H. *The Parables of the Kingdom*. New York: Scribners, 1961.

Dorsey, Thomas A. *Take My Hand Precious Lord*. Chicago: Hill and Range Songs, 1938.

Doyle, Arthur Conan. *The Sign of Four*. London: Spencer Blackett, 1890.

Duck, Ruth C. *Gender and the Name of God: The Trinitarian Baptismal Formula*. New York: Pilgrim Press, 1991.

Dunan-Page, Anne, ed. *The Cambridge Companion to Bunyan*. New York: Cambridge University Press, 2010.

Elliott, J. K., ed. *The Apocryphal Jesus: Legends of the Early Church*. New York: Oxford University Press, 1996.

Ellis, Christopher J. *Gathering: A Theology and Spirituality of Worship in Free Church Tradition*. London: SCM Press, 2004.

Ellsberg, Robert. *All Saints: Daily Reflections on Saints, Prophets, and Witnesses for Our Time*. New York: Crossroad, 2004.

Emerson, Matthew Y. *He Descended into the Dead: An Evangelical Theology of Holy Saturday*. Downers Grove, IL: InterVarsity, 2019.

English Language Liturgical Commission (ELLC). *Praying Together*. Nashville: Abingdon Press, 1988.

Episcopal Church. *The Book of Common Prayer*. New York: Church Publishing, 2007.

Eusebius. "Church History." Translated by Arthur Cushman McGiffert. In *The Nicene and Post-Nicene Fathers*, Second Series, edited by Henry Wace and Philip Schaff, 81–387. Vol. 1. Grand Rapids, MI: Eerdmans, 1976.

Fackre, Gabriel. *The Christian Story: A Narrative Interpretation of Christian Doctrine*. Rev. ed. Grand Rapids, MI: Eerdmans, 1984.

Ferguson, Everett. *Early Christians Speak: Faith and Life in the First Three Centuries*. Austin, TX: Sweet Publishing, 1971.

———. "Irenaeus' Proof of the Apostolic Preaching and Early Catechetical Instruction." In *The Early Church at Work and*

Worship. Vol. 2: *Catechesis, Baptism, Eschatology, and Martyrdom*. Eugene, OR: Cascade, 2014.

Fiddes, Paul S. "Dual Citizenship in Athens and Jerusalem: The Place of the Christian Scholar in the Life of the Church." In *Questions of Identity: Essays in Honour of Brian Haymes*. Centre for Baptist History and Heritage Studies 6, edited by Anthony R. Cross and Ruth M. B. Gouldbourne. Oxford: Regent's Park College, 2011.

Finn, Thomas M. *Early Christian Baptism and the Catechumenate: Italy, North Africa, and Egypt*. Collegeville, MN: Liturgical Press, 1992.

———. *Early Christian Baptism and the Catechumenate: West and East Syria*. Collegeville, MN: Liturgical Press, 1992.

Flannery, Austin, ed. *Vatican Council II: Volume 1, The Conciliar and Postconciliar Documents*. Rev. ed. Northport, NY: Costello Publishing Company, 2004.

Fosdick, Harry Emerson. *Dear Mr. Brown: Letters to a Person Perplexed about Religion*. New York: Harper & Row, 1961.

Fowl, Stephen E. and L. Gregory Jones. *Reading in Communion: Scripture and Ethics in Christian Life*. Grand Rapids, MI: Eerdmans, 1991.

Freeman, Curtis W. "Can Baptist Theology Be Revisioned?" *Perspectives in Religious Studies* 24, no. 3 (1997): 273–310.

———. *Contesting Catholicity: Theology for Other Baptists*. Waco, TX: Baylor University Press, 2014.

———. "God in Three Persons: Baptist Unitarianism and the Trinity." *Perspectives in Religious Studies* 33, no. 3 (2006): 323–44.

———. *Pilgrim Letters: Instruction in the Basic Teaching of Christ*. Minneapolis: Fortress Press, 2021.

———. "Toward a *Sensus Fidelium* for an Evangelical Church." In *The Nature of Confession: Evangelicals and Postliberal in Conversation*, edited by Timothy R. Phillips and Dennis L. Okholm. Downers Grove, IL: InterVarsity Press, 1996.

———. *Undomesticated Dissent: Democracy and the Public Virtue of Religious Nonconformity*. Waco, TX: Baylor University Press, 2017.

Frei, Hans W. *The Eclipse of Biblical Narrative: A Study in Eigh-teenth and Nineteenth Century Hermeneutics*. New Haven, CT: Yale University Press, 1974.

————. *The Identity of Jesus Christ: The Hermeneutical Bases of Dogmatic Theology*. Eugene, OR: Wipf & Stock, 1997.

Frye, Northrop. *Northrop Frye in Conversation*. Edited by David Cayley. Concord, ON: Anansi, 1992.

German Baptist Union/Bund Evangelisch-Freikirchlicher Ge-meinden. *Rechenschaft vom Glauben*. Accessed July 23, 2022. https://www.baptisten.de/fileadmin/bgs/media/doku mente/Rechenschaft_vom_Glauben_-_Stand_31.05 .2019.pdf.

Gogarten, Friedrich. *Von Glauben und Offenbarung, Vier Vor-träge*. Jena: Eugen Diederichs, 1923.

Goldberg, Michael. *Jews and Christians Getting Our Stories Straight: The Exodus and the Passion-Resurrection*. Nashville: Abingdon, 1985.

Green, Bernard. *European Baptists and the Third Reich*. Didcot: Baptist Historical Society, 1997.

Greene-McCreight, Kathryn. "Feminist Liturgical Trinities and a Generous Orthodoxy." In *The Place of Christ in Liturgical Prayer*, edited by Brian D. Spinks. Collegeville, MN: Litur-gical Press, 2008.

————. "When I Say God, I Mean Father, Son and Holy Spirit: On the Ecumenical Baptismal Formula." *Pro Ecclesia* 6, no. 3 (Summer 1997): 289–308.

Gregory of Nazianzus. "Orations." Translated by Charles Gor-don Browne and James Edward Swallow. In *The Nicene and Post-Nicene Fathers*, Second Series, edited by Philip Schaff and Henry Wace, 203–434. Vol. 7. Grand Rapids, MI: Eerdmans, 1976.

Gregory of Nyssa. *The Life of Moses*. Translated by Abraham J. Malherbe and Everett Ferguson. New York: Paulist Press, 1978.

Grice, Homer L. *The Daily Vacation Bible School Guide*. Nash-ville: Southern Baptist Sunday School Board, 1926.

Grudem, Wayne. "He Did Not Descend into Hell: A Plea for Following Scripture Instead of the Apostles' Creed." *Journal*

of the Evangelical Theological Society 34, no. 1 (March 1991):
103–13.

———. Systematic Theology: An Introduction to Biblical Doctrine.
Grand Rapids, MI: Zondervan, 1994.

Hartshorne, Charles. The Divine Relativity: A Social Conception of
God. New Haven, CT: Yale University Press, 1948.

Hastings, Selina, Countess of Huntingdon, ed. A Select Collection
of Hymns. 5th ed. London: Hughes and Walsh, 1780.

Hauerwas, Stanley. The Work of Theology. Grand Rapids, MI:
Eerdmans, 2015.

Haykin, Michael A. G. Amidst Us Our Belovèd Stands: Recovering
Sacrament in the Baptist Tradition. Bellingham, WA: Lexham Press, 2022.

Hays, Richard B. Echoes of Scripture in the Letters of Paul. New
Haven, CT: Yale University Press, 1989.

———. Reading Backwards: Figural Christology and the Fourfold
Gospel Witness. Waco, TX: Baylor University Press, 2016.

Herbert, Paula. "Nonsexist Language." The Washington Post, May
28, 1983. Accessed September 13, 2022. https://www
.washingtonpost.com/archive/local/1983/05/28/nonsexist
-language/4cbb8cce-76b3–4fae-8070–3aac1ed3e9aa/.

Heschel, Abraham Joshua. God in Search of Man. New York: Farrar, Strauss and Giroux, 1955.

———. Sabbath: Its Meaning for Modern Man. New York: Farrar,
Straus and Giroux, 2005.

Hickman, Hoyt L., Don E. Saliers, Laurence Hull Stookey, and
James F. White. The New Handbook of the Christian Year.
Nashville: Abingdon, 1992.

Hill, Preston. "When Jesus Doubted God: Perspectives from
Calvin on Post-Traumatic Faith." The Other Journal, February
10, 2022. Accessed July 12, 2022. https://theotherjournal
.com/2022/02/10/doubt-calvin-post-traumatic-faith/.

Hippolytus. The Treatise on the Apostolic Tradition of St. Hippolytus of Rome. Edited by Gregory Dix and Henry Chadwick.
London: Alban Press, 1992.

Houtchens, Lawrence, and Carolyn Washburn Houtchens, ed.
The English Romantic Poets and Essayists. New York: Modern
Language Association, 1957.

Hudson, Virginia Cary. *O Ye Jigs & Juleps!* New York: Macmillan, 1962.

Hügel, Friedrich von. *Essays and Addresses on the Philosophy of Religion*. London: J. M. Dent, 1924.

Ignatius of Antioch. "The Letters of Ignatius," Edited and translated by Cyril C. Richardson. In *Early Christian Fathers*, *The Library of Christian Classics*, 74–120. Vol. 1. New York: Collier Books, 1970.

Irenaeus. *The Proof of the Apostolic Preaching*. Translated by Armitage Robinson. New York: Macmillan, 1920.

James, E. S. "The Invincible Gospel." Sermon preached at the 1941 Baptist General Convention of Texas. Vernon, TX: First Baptist Church, n.d.

Jefferson, Thomas. *The Papers of Thomas Jefferson*. Princeton, NJ: Princeton University Press, 1950.

———. *The Papers of Thomas Jefferson Digital Edition*. Edited by James P. McClure and J. Jefferson Looney. Charlottesville: University of Virginia Press, Rotunda, 2008–2022. Accessed July 30, 2022. https://rotunda-upress-virginia-edu.proxy.lib.duke.edu/founders/TSJN-01-40-02-0178-0001.

Jennings, Willie James. *The Christian Imagination: Theology and the Origins of Race*. New Haven, CT: Yale University Press, 2010.

Jenson, Robert W. *Systematic Theology, Volume 1: The Triune God*. New York: Oxford, 1997.

Jerome. "The Homilies of Saint Jerome." Translated by Marie Liguori Ewald. In *The Fathers of the Church*, edited by Roy Joseph Deferrari. Vol. 57. Washington, DC: The Catholic University of America Press, 1966.

Johnson, Elizabeth A. *She Who Is: The Mystery of God in Feminist Theological Discourse*. New York: Crossroad, 1992.

Johnson, James Weldon. *God's Trombones*. New York: Penguin Books, 1976.

Johnson, Maxwell E. *Rites of Christian Initiation: Their Evolution and Interpretation*. 2nd ed. Collegeville, MN: Liturgical Press, 2007.

Jüngel, Eberhard. *God as the Mystery of the World*. Translated by Darrell L. Guder. London: Bloomsbury, 1983.

Justin Martyr. "Dialogue with Trypho." Translated by Marcus
    Dods and George Reith. In *The Ante-Nicene Fathers*, edited
    by Alexander Roberts, James Donaldson, and A. Cleveland
    Coxe, 194–270. Vol. 1. Grand Rapids, MI: Eerdmans,
    1950.

Kaufman, Gordon D. *God the Problem*. Cambridge, MA: Har-
    vard University Press, 1972.

Kay, James F. "In Whose Name?: Feminism and the Trinitar-
    ian Baptismal Formula." *Theology Today* 49, no. 4 (January
    1993): 524–33.

Kelly, J. N. D. *Early Christian Creeds*. 3rd ed. New York: Long-
    man, 1972.

Kelsey, David H. *Proving Doctrine: The Uses of Scripture in Mod-
    ern Theology*. Harrisburg, PA: Trinity Press, 1999.

Kermode, Frank. *The Sense of an Ending: Studies in the Theory of
    Fiction*. New York: Oxford, 1966.

Kiffin, William. *A Sober Discourse of Right to Church Commu-
    nion*. London: George Larkin, 1681.

Kolb, Robert, and James A. Nestingen. *Sources and Contexts of
    The Book of Concord*. Minneapolis: Fortress Press, 2001.

Kreider, Alan. *The Change of Conversion and the Origin of Chris-
    tendom*. Harrisburg, PA: Trinity Press, 1999.

Langland, William. *Piers Plowman* (The C Version). Translated
    by George Economou. Philadelphia: University of Pennsyl-
    vania Press, 1996.

Lash, Nicholas. *Easter in Ordinary: Reflections on Human Experi-
    ence and the Knowledge of God*. Charlottesville: University of
    Virginia Press, 1988.

———. *Theology on the Way to Emmaus*. London: SCM Press,
    1986.

Lathrop, Gordon W. *Holy Things: A Liturgical Theology*. Minne-
    apolis: Fortress, 1998.

Leclecq, Jean. *The Love of Learning and the Desire for God*. Trans-
    lated by Cathearine Misrahi. New York: Fordham Univer-
    sity Press, 1982.

Levine, Amy-Jill. "Go and Do Likewise: Lessons from the Para-
    ble of the Good Samaritan." *America: The Jesuit Review* 211,
    no. 8 (September 29, 2014): 16–18.

———. "The Many Faces of the Good Samaritan—Mostly Wrong." *Biblical Archaeology Review* 38, no. 1 (2012): 24, 68.

Lewis, C. S. *The Lion, the Witch, and the Wardrobe*. New York: Macmillan, 1988.

Lindbeck, George A. "The Bible as Realistic Narrative." *Journal of Ecumenical Studies* 17, no. 1 (1980): 81–85.

———. *The Church in a Postliberal Age*. Edited by James J. Buckley. Grand Rapids, MI: Eerdmans, 2002.

Lombard, Peter. *The Sentences*. 4 vols. Translated by Giulio Silano. Toronto: Pontifical Institute of Mediaeval Studies, 2007–2010.

Louth, Andrew. *Discerning the Mystery: An Essay on the Nature of Theology*. Oxford: Clarendon Press, 1983.

Lubac, Henri de. *Medieval Exegesis: The Four Senses of Scripture*. 3 vols. Translated by Mark Sebanc and E. M. Macierowski. Grand Rapids, MI: Eerdmans, 1998–2000.

———. *The Mystery of the Supernatural*. London: G. Chapman, 1967.

———. *The Sources of Revelation*. Translated by Luke O'Neill. New York: Herder and Herder, 1968.

———. *Theological Fragments*. Translated by Rebecca Howell Balinski. San Francisco: Ignatius, 1989.

Lumpkin, William L. *Baptist Confessions of Faith*. Rev. ed. Valley Forge, PA: Judson Press, 1969.

Luther, Martin. "The Babylonian Captivity of the Church." Translated by A. T. W. Steinhäuser and revised by Frederick C. Ahrens and Abdel Ross Wentz. In *Luther's Works*, edited by Helmut T. Lehmann, 11–126. Vol. 36. Philadelphia: Fortress, 1959.

———. "The Bondage of the Will." Translated by Philip S. Watson. In *Luther's Works*, edited by Helmut T. Lehmann. Vol. 33. Philadelphia: Fortress, 1972.

———. "The Estate of Marriage." Translated by Walther I. Brandt. In *Luther's Works*, edited by Helmut T. Lehmann, 11–49. Vol. 45. Philadelphia: Fortress, 1962.

———. "Heidelberg Disputation." Translated by Harold J. Grimm. In *Luther's Works*, edited by Helmut T. Lehmann, 39–70. Vol. 31. Philadelphia: Fortress, 1957.

———. "Lectures on Genesis." chapters 26–30. Translated by George V. Schick and Paul D. Pahl. In *Luther's Works*, edited by Jaroslav Pelikan and Walter A. Hansen. Vol. 5. St. Louis: Concordia Publishing House, 1968.

———. "On the Councils and the Church." Translated by Charles M. Jacobs and revised by Eric W. Gritsch. In *Luther's Works*, Helmut T. Lehmann, 3–178. Vol. 41. Philadelphia: Fortress, 1966.

———. *Select Works of Martin Luther*. 4 vols. Translated by Henry Cole. London: T. Bensley, 1826.

MacIntyre, Alasdair, *After Virtue*. Notre Dame, IN: University of Notre Dame Press, 1981.

Marcel, Gabriel. *Being and Having*. Translated by Katharine Farrer. Westminster: Dacre Press, 1949.

Marcus, Joel. *Mark 1–8*. Vol. 27 in *The Anchor Bible*. New York: Doubleday, 2000.

Martyn, J. Louis. *Galatians*. Vol. 33A in *The Anchor Yale Bible*. New Haven, CT: Yale University Press, 1997.

Mavrodes, George I. "Some Puzzles Concerning Omnipotence." *Philosophical Review* 72, no. 2 (1963): 221–23.

McCabe, Herbert. *God Matters*. London: Geoffrey Chapman, 1987.

McClendon, James Wm., Jr. "Atonement, Discipleship and Freedom." *Baptist Student* 44 (November 1964): 50–58.

———. *Doctrine: Systematic Theology, Volume II*. Waco, TX: Baylor University Press, 2012.

———. *Ethics: Systematic Theology, Volume I*. Waco, TX: Baylor University Press, 2012.

———. *Witness: Systematic Theology, Volume III*. Waco, TX: Baylor University Press, 2012.

Mead, Loren B. *The Once and Future Church: Reinventing the Congregation for a New Mission Frontier*. Washington, DC: Alban, 1991.

Melitio of Sardis. *On Pascha*. Translated by Alistair Stewart-Sykes. Yonkers, NY: St. Vladimir's Seminary Press, 2001.

Merriman, Michael W., ed. *The Baptismal Mystery and the Catechumenate*. New York: Church Publishing, 1990.

Milton, John. *On the Morning of Christ's Nativity.* Cambridge, UK: Cambridge University Press, 1923.

Moltmann, Jürgen. *The Crucified God: The Cross of Christ as the Foundation and Criticism of Christian Theology.* Translated by R. A. Wilson and John Bowden. New York: Harper, 1974.

———. *God in Creation: A New Theology of Creation and the Spirit of God.* Translated by Margaret Kohl. Minneapolis: Fortress, 1993.

Morris, Thomas H. *The RCIA: Transforming the Church.* New York: Paulist Press, 1997.

Mulhall, Stephen. *The Great Riddle: Wittgenstein and Nonsense, Theology and Philosophy.* Oxford: Oxford University Press, 2015.

Niebuhr, H. Richard. "The Doctrine of the Trinity and the Unity of the Church." *Theology Today* 3, no. 3 (1946): 371–84.

Norris, Kathleen. *Quotidian Mysteries: Laundry, Liturgy, and "Women's Work."* Mahwah, NJ: Paulist Press, 1998.

Norris, R. A., Jr., ed. *The Christological Controversy.* Philadelphia: Fortress, 1980.

"Nuns on the Run." Directed by Jonathan Lynn, March 30, 1990, London: HandMade Films, 1990, Video.

Origen, "Homilies on Luke." Translated by Joseph T. Lienhard. In *The Fathers of the Church,* edited by Thomas Halton. Vol. 94. Washington, DC: The Catholic University of America Press, 1996.

Otto, Rudolf. *The Idea of the Holy.* 2nd ed. Translated by John W. Harvey. London: Oxford, 1958.

Packer, J. I. *Knowing God.* Downers Grove, IL: InterVarsity, 1973.

Packer, J. I., and Gary A. Parrett. *Grounded in the Gospel: Building Believers the Old-Fashioned Way.* Grand Rapids, MI: Baker, 2010.

Parker, G. Keith. *Baptists in Europe: History and Confessions of Faith.* Nashville: Broadman, 1982.

Payne, Ernest. *The Fellowship of Believers: Baptist Thought and Practice, Yesterday and Today.* 2nd ed. London: Carey Kingsgate, 1952.

Pelikan, Jaroslav, and Valerie Hotchkiss, eds. *Creeds and Confession of Faith in the Christian Tradition.* 4 vols. New Haven, CT: Yale University Press, 2004.

Peters, Ted. *God as Trinity: Relationality and Temporality in Divine Life.* Louisville, KY: Westminster/John Knox, 1993.

Peterson, Eugene H. *A Long Obedience in the Same Direction: Discipleship in an Instant Society.* Downers Grove, IL: InterVarsity Press, 1980.

Peifer, Jane Hoober, and John Stahl-Wert. *Welcoming New Christians: A Guide for the Christian Initiation of Adults.* Newton, KS: Faith and Life Press; Scottdale, PA: Mennonite Publishing House, 1995.

Philips, Dietrich. "The Church of God." In *Spiritual and Anabaptist Writers, The Library of Christian Classics*, edited by George H. Williams, 226–60. Vol. 25. Philadelphia: Westminster Press, 1957.

Presbyterian Church (USA), *Book of Confessions.* Revised study ed. Louisville, KY: Westminster/John Knox Press, 2017.

Preus, James S. *From Shadow to Promise: Old Testament Interpretation from Augustine to the Young Luther.* Cambridge, MA: Harvard University Press, 1969.

Rahner, Karl. *The Theology of the Spiritual Life.* Translated by Karl H. Kruger and Boniface Kruger. In *Theological Investigations.* Vol. 3. Baltimore: Helicon, 1967.

Rippon, John, ed. *A Selection of Hymns.* London: Thomas Wilkins, 1787.

Robinson, John. *The Works of John Robinson: Pastor of the Pilgrim Fathers.* Edited by Robert Ashton. 3 vols. London: John Snow, 1851.

Sarisky, Darren, ed. *Theologies of Retrieval: An Exploration and Appraisal.* New York: Bloomsbury T & T Clark, 2017.

Schaff, Philip. *The Creeds of Christendom.* 6th ed. 3 vols. New York: Harper, 1931.

Schmemann, Alexander. *For the Life of the World: Sacraments and Orthodoxy.* Crestwood, NY: St. Vladimir's Seminary Press, 2004.

Schmid, Konrad, and Jens Schröter. *The Making of the Bible: From the First Fragments to Sacred Scripture*. Translated by Peter Lewis. Cambridge, MA: Belknap Press, 2021.

Schwartz, Martin. "Preaching in the Basel Prison." In *Karl Barth in der Strafanstalt*. Translated by Joseph Longarino. Center for Barth Studies, Princeton Theological Seminary. Accessed July 9, 2022. https://barth.ptsem.edu/preaching-in-the-basel-prison/.

Seitz, Christopher R. *The Character of Christian Scripture: The Significance of a Two-Testament Bible*. Grand Rapids, MI: Baker Academic, 2011.

Senn, Frank C. *A Stewardship of the Mysteries*. Mahwah, NJ: Paulist Press, 1999.

"The Seven Ecumenical Councils." Translated by Henry R. Percival. In *The Nicene and Post-Nicene Fathers*, Second Series, edited by Philip Schaff and Henry Wace. Vol. 14. Grand Rapids, MI: Eerdmans, 1977.

Smith, James K. A. *You Are What You Love: The Spiritual Power of Habit*. Grand Rapids, MI: Brazos, 2016.

Smyth, John. *The Works of John Smyth*. Edited by W. T. Whitley. 2 vols. Cambridge, UK: Cambridge University Press, 1915.

Soskice, Janet Martin. *The Kindness of God: Metaphor, Gender, and Religious Language*. New York: Oxford, 2007.

———. *Metaphor and Religious Language*. New York: Clarendon Press, 1985.

Soulen, R. Kendall. *The God of Israel and Christian Theology*. Minneapolis: Fortress, 1996.

Sozomenus. "Church History." Translated by Chester D. Hartranft. In *The Nicene and Post-Nicene Fathers*, Second Series, edited by Philip Schaff and Henry Wace, 179–427. Vol. 2. Grand Rapids, MI: Eerdmans, 1973.

Spurgeon, C. H. *Lectures to My Students*. Grand Rapids, MI: Zondervan, 1962.

Steinmetz, David C. *Memory and Mission: Theological Reflections on the Christian Past*. Nashville: Abingdon, 1988.

————. "Luther and the Ascent of Jacob's Ladder." *Church History* 55, no. 2 (1986): 179–92.

Strahan, Joshua. *The Basics of Christian Belief: Bible, Theology, and Life's Big Questions*. Grand Rapids, MI: Baker, 2020.

Talley, Thomas J. *The Origins of the Liturgical Year*. New York: Pueblo Publishing, 1986.

Tertullian. "Apology." Translated by S. Thelwall. In *The Ante-Nicene Fathers*, edited by A. Cleveland Coxe, 17–60. Vol. 3. Grand Rapids, MI: Eerdmans, 1978.

Tilley, Terrence W. *The Disciples' Jesus: Christology as Reconciling Practice*. Maryknoll, NY: Orbis Books, 2008.

Tolkien, J. R. R. *Tree and Leaf*. London: Unwin Books, 1964.

Torrance, James B. *Worship Community and the Triune God of Grace*. Downers Grove, IL: InterVarsity Press, 1996.

Torrence, Thomas F. *Incarnation: The Person and Life of Christ*. Edited by Robert T. Walker. Downers Grove, IL: InterVarsity, 2008.

Turner, Denys. *The Darkness of God: Negativity in Christian Mysticism*. Cambridge, UK: Cambridge University Press, 1995.

Vanhoozer, Kevin J. *The Drama of Doctrine: A Canonical-Linguistic Approach to Christian Theology*. Louisville, KY: Westminster/John Knox, 2005.

————. "A Drama of Redemption Model." In *Four Views on Moving beyond the Bible to Theology*, edited by Gary T. Meadors. Grand Rapids, MI: Zondervan, 2009.

Voragine, Jacobus de. *The Golden Legend or Lives of the Saints*. Translated by William Caxton. In *Temple Classics*, edited by F. S. Ellis. 7 vols. London: J. M. Dent, 1900.

Warner, Anna Bartlett. *Say and Seal*. 2 vols. Philadelphia: Lippincott, 1880.

Webb, Stephen H. "Why von Balthasar Was Wrong about Holy Saturday." *First Things*, August 27, 2013, web exclusive. Accessed July 9, 2022. https://www.firstthings.com/web-exclusives/2013/08/why-von-balthasar-was-wrong-about-holy-saturday.

Webber, Robert E. *Ancient-Future Faith: Rethinking Evangelicalism for a Postmodern World*. Grand Rapids, MI: Baker, 1999.

———. *Ancient-Future Time: Forming Spirituality through the Christian Year*. Grand Rapids, MI: Baker, 2004.

———. *Journey to Jesus: The Worship, Evangelism, and Nurture Mission of the Church*. Nashville: Abingdon, 2001.

Wehner, Peter. "The Evangelical Church Is Breaking Apart." *The Atlantic*, October 24, 2021. Accessed August 29, 2022. https://www.theatlantic.com/ideas/archive/2021/10/evangelical-trump-christians-politics/620469.

Weil, Simone. "Spiritual Autobiography." In *Waiting for God*. Translated by Emma Craufurd. New York: HarperCollins, 1973.

Wells, Samuel. *Improvisation: The Drama of Christian Ethics*. Grand Rapids, MI: Brazos Press, 2004.

West, Cornell. *Prophesy Deliverance! An Afro-American Revolutionary Christianity*. Philadelphia: Westminster Press, 1982.

Wilken, Robert L. "The Lives of the Saints and the Pursuit of Virtue." *First Things* 1, no. 8 (December 1990): 45–51.

Wilkinson, John, ed. and trans. *Egeria's Travels to the Holy Land*. Rev. ed. Jerusalem: Ariel Publishing, 1981.

Williams, Dewey. *Finding Joy on Death Row: Unexpected Lessons from Lives We Discarded*. Nashville: Dexterity Press, 2023.

Winslow, Edward. *Hypocrisie Unmasked*. London: Rich. Cotes, 1646. Reprint New York: Burt Franklin, 1968.

Wirzba, Norman. *Living the Sabbath: Discovering the Rhythms of Rest and Delight*. Grand Rapids, MI: Brazos Press, 2006.

Wren, Brian. *What Language Shall I Borrow?: God-Talk in Worship: A Male Response to Feminist Theology*. New York: Crossroad, 1990.

Wright, N. T. "How Can the Bible Be Authoritative?" *Vox Evangelica* 21 (1991): 7–32.

———. *The New Testament and the People of God*. Minneapolis: Fortress, 1992.

Yarnell, Malcolm B., III. *God the Trinity: Biblical Portraits*. Nashville: Broadman and Holman, 2016.

Topical Index

Scripture Index